D0594164
P H 22
STRAND PRICE
5 00

CONVERGE

CONVERGE

TRANSFORMING BUSINESS AT THE INTERSECTION OF MARKETING AND TECHNOLOGY

BOB LORD
RAY VELEZ

WILEY

Cover image: John Wiley & Sons, Inc.
Cover design: Bett Hallonquist, Atomic Design Lab

Published by John Wiley & Sons, Inc., Hoboken, New Jersey.
Published simultaneously in Canada.

Library of Congress Cataloging-in-Publication Data:

Lord, Bob, 1963-

Converge: transforming business at the intersection of marketing and technology/ Bob Lord, Ray Velez.

pages cm

Includes index.

ISBN 978-1-118-57552-9 (cloth); ISBN 978-1-118-63224-6 (ebk);

ISBN 978-1-118-63222-2 (ebk); ISBN 978-1-118-63209-3 (ebk)

1. Business. 2. Marketing. 3. Technological innovations. I. Velez, Ray, 1969- II. Title.

HF1008.L67 2013

658.4'062—dc23

2012049840

Printed in the United States of America

10 9 8 7 6 5 4 3 2 1

Contents

Foreword

This book is insightful, relevant, and will appeal to anyone with an interest in marketing products and managing successful, sustainable businesses.

Bob and Ray set out their arguments for the convergence of creativity, technology, and media—simply and unambiguously. They make us think differently about marketing and about business. They help us understand what's going on and how to survive in the evolving world of consumer-selection.

Creativity, technology, and media all serve to enrich the consumer experience. They have always done so in their, hitherto, largely separate ways.

But the convergence that is so well described in this book makes us challenge traditional assumptions about what we do, how we do it, and how we are organized.

Theirs is a world where success depends on getting rid of silos; where there is a coming together, a process of joined-up thinking on a massive scale recognizing the connectedness of things.

The democratization of data and of creativity, cross-disciplinary thinking, and next-generation storytelling present a compelling vision of the changes organizations must make if they are to succeed.

I have witnessed these trends in my own company. Increasingly, evolving consumer behaviors are requiring us to develop a more coordinated ecosystem of activity.

In particular, the proliferation of mobile technology globally is building an intense, always-on, one-to-one relationship between brands, businesses, and consumers. This is already having a profound effect on how we *converge* the strands of our marketing activity.

In our quest for sustainable growth, Unilever recognizes that its entire business model must change, and in order to lead, must adapt to a new, converging world.

We know we cannot deliver sustainable growth on our own. We must share ideas, develop partnerships, collaborate, cocreate solutions, and reimagine our brands in terms of the long-term benefits they bring to our consumers, society, and the planet.

Organizationally, we have brought together marketing, communications, and sustainability under one leadership at the global board level and are working through the ways that these *converge*. Our challenge is to build an operating model that can turn this complexity into a source of sustainable competitive advantage. In this hyperconnected world that feeds off data, I now feel that I am as likely to talk about my business in terms of cloud formations as I am organization charts.

The concept of convergence is game changing. As you read *Converge*, free your mind and ask yourself, Are my organization and I ready to face the challenges that it says I must in order to succeed?

—**Keith Weed**, Chief Marketing
and Communication Officer,
Unilever plc

Introduction

This is a book about how to succeed in a business environment in which creativity, technology, and media are coming closer together, a convergence that's happening at the speed of sound. We'll explore these trends, and we'll describe the changes your business needs to make in order to take advantage of them. At its core this book is about innovation and success, about the present and the future. But before we can go on and plunge ahead, we need to look at where we've been.

Our story begins in 2002, anything but a banner year for most global businesses, not least the then seven-year-old Razorfish. Post-9/11 uncertainty was heavy in the air. Business sections looked like crime blotters, dominated as they were by the fallout from Enron, WorldCom, Tyco, and other corporate scandals. *Forbes* counted 22 accounting scandals alone that year, and that's not including insider trading and other bad behavior. Making matters worse for Razorfish, no one quite knew what to make of this whole Internet thing. The entrepreneurial fires the growth of the Web had lit just a few years before had been stamped out by the collapse of the house of cards that was the Internet boom of the late 1990s.

In our corner of the world, the Internet consulting and agency business, things were more than a little jittery. In addition to killing off new economy pretenders such as Pets.com, Webvan, and eToys, the dot-com bust had wiped out a lot of enthusiasm about the Internet. The decline of dot-com challengers meant that many *Fortune 500* businesses had scaled back on consulting. In the marketing world, there was much the same story. By the end of 2002, online advertising, already just a drop in the spending bucket, was down more than 13 percent. The idea that the Internet was just a fad whose time was come was spreading through the business world. Our company, Razorfish, which had grown up with the dot-com craze, was not immune.

Formed in 1995 in a New York City bedroom, the funnily named Razorfish represented all the excitement and excesses of the time. Its founders brandished expensive clothes, boasted celebrity friends, and even owned a nightclub. They were brash and irreverent spokesmen for a new wave of business thinking that was trying to wrap its mind around the Internet. They were featured in outlets from *60 Minutes* to *Wired,* whose term for them, "New Media Peacocks" both summed up their craving for the spotlight and the intense media skepticism around the company. Ahead of their time, they often lacked the vocabulary—and the media training—to capture in words all the value the company was bringing to clients, even in those early days. The *60 Minutes* segment aired the famous exchange between cofounder Jeff Dachis and CBS correspondent Bob Simon when Dachis declared, "We have asked our clients to recontextualize their business." Simon balked at the use of the r-word and demanded, "Tell me what you do—in English." (An account of this interchange appears in *Wired,* September 2000.)

Yet blue-chip clients seeking new voices who could help them understand the Internet hired us. Offering a mix of business strategy, technology, and design, Razorfish won clients like Ford Motor Co., Giorgio Armani, and Charles Schwab, turning the company into a major concern in just a few years. Partaking in the era's initial public offering (IPO) fever, Razorfish went public in April 1999, raising $48 million. The stock, initially priced at $16, closed on the first day of trading at $38, a pop that was evidence of the insanity that had taken hold of the markets. By 2000, after a string of acquisitions, Razorfish had 1,800 employees in 13 global cities. But within a year, the Internet bubble deflated and the decline began. The NASDQ composite, which touched a high of over 5,000 in March 2000, was below 1,200 by late September 2002—more than three-quarters of its value erased. In November 2002,

Razorfish, with just 230 employees and stock that was trading for less than $2, was sold—for the less-than-princely sum of $8.2 million.

For some companies in some industries, this would have been the end of the road. When the party ends, the company with the funny name and more PR than revenue gets bought up on the cheap and chopped up for parts, a story that had become familiar during the dot-com wipeout. And our case didn't seem like an exception. In an interview at the time, Ned Stringham, the chief executive officer (CEO) of SBI Group, Razorfish's new owner, summed up the level of enthusiasm for the brand: "We're going to continue using Razorfish for a little while longer."

But this was far from the end of the line for Razorfish.

Indeed, even in those dark days, there were positive developments that, more than just keeping the lights on at our company pointed the way to the future in which we would not only survive but thrive. In particular, there were a couple of client engagements that demonstrated to us that the Internet was far from a fad and that if used properly it could be an amazing way to connect with your consumers.

First, there was Cisco Systems, whose routers and switches had powered the Internet boom. Despite its vital importance to the Web, Cisco Systems had hit the same tough stretch the rest of the tech world did in 2002. Just two years earlier, Cisco was the most valuable company in the world measured in terms of market capitalization. But after making the largest write-down in history in 2001, it was facing plummeting demand for its hardware as technology spending was cut.

There was another problem. Cisco's global Web presence, the front door of the company for customers all over the world, was tough to use. It had been built around the vast company's many business units, not for customer use. To put it simply, if you were looking to buy a router or a switch—Cisco's core business—it wasn't easy to figure out where to go. Aware of the problem, Cisco asked us to redesign its corporate website to add a deeper layer of intelligence and interaction that was more oriented around how customers can manage and solve problems. We built a content management system that was grounded in what Cisco's resellers needed and delivered the relevant product information based on sellers' vertical industries.

Now it might sound straightforward, but back then it was anything but. No agency in the world could do what we did, nor could any technology company. Why? Because you needed to know both the business plan and the marketing plan and understand how to deploy technology to bring the two together. At its base, the assignment was about shaping a digital asset for customers' needs, not the company's silos.

The second telling assignment was for a very different kind of company. Where Cisco was a huge enterprise, Major League Baseball's Advanced Media (MLB.com) was anything but advanced. A spin-off of the 130-year-old league, MLB.com was housed not at MLB's posh Park Avenue headquarters but in Chelsea Market, across the street from where Google would set up shop years later. Back then, Chelsea Market wasn't the boho mix of work and play it is now, where cute food shops, restaurants, and coffee shops feed well-heeled office dwellers. Back then, rats and other pests roamed the office. One night, an MLB.com executive who had pulled an all-nighter and slept on the floor awoke with fleabites. But roughing it made sense when you consider that MLB.com was effectively an in-house startup.

MLB.com was created in 2000, with a focus of tying together and monetizing its digital assets. In a major coup, the League had convinced all of its 30 clubs to cede their digital rights to MLB.com. To understand the importance of this, think of the 30 teams that make up Major League baseball as 30 different operating subsidiaries, each with its distinct history and culture. Many of them are bitter enemies with grudges that go way back. In other words, this required nothing less than getting the Red Sox and the Yankees on the same page. But they did it.

The next step was creating the consumer experience, a job for which MLB hired Scient, an agency which would eventually be rolled up into Razorfish. The team developed the overall website infrastructure and the ticketing infrastructure, as well as the streaming media. For the time, it was a massive success. As one article summed up: "The grand old game has brought itself to the point where it can face the same challenge as thousands of other big businesses: how to harness the Web channel for revenue, marketing, and enhanced customer experiences . . . at least Major League Baseball finally recognizes the Internet as a channel to serve the one part of the sport that ultimately matters most: the fan."

Substitute the word *customer* for *fan,* and you'll understand the central kernel of this book. What MLB understood from just about the dawn of the Web is that the customer comes first and your business silos and organizational charts, not to mention egos, are way down the line. Engage the customer with the right technologically enabled creativity and you'll provide experiences that not only keep them coming back but really ring the register. And the benefits of that outlook are clearer than ever, as MLB has continued to innovate. Its MLB.TV, a subscription service that broadcasts all games, has been a hit. By 2012, MLB.com was bringing in about $620 million from tickets, mobile apps, and streaming subscriptions, according to an article in *Fast Company*. If it had gone public as its owners had discussed, the article stated, the IPO would have been worth about $2.5 billion. "Baseball's digital arm," the author wrote, "has quietly proven itself to be New York's top tech startup of the last decade."

In both instances, we saw how marketing, media, and technology were all coming together and we saw how important it was for consumer-facing companies to be ready for it. Cisco needed to think past its organizational prejudices to create a Web presence that made sense to customers; MLB needed to get its various stakeholders on board to create a consumer-centric experience rather than a fragmented one. Now its content is available wherever consumers are: on computers, tablets, and mobile phones, on Apple TV, Roku, and Xbox.

Crucially, MLB and Cisco validated our own positioning at a time when many naysayers were telling us that we had to make a choice between being a technology company or a marketing company. There was no room, the criticism went both externally, and internally, for a company that tried to do it "all." At the time, we suspected this was a false dichotomy. Years later, we know it was.

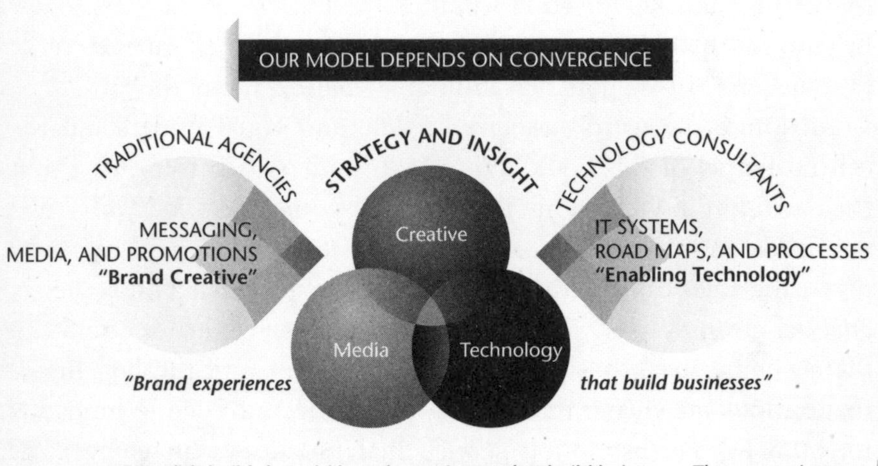

Razorfish builds brands' brand experiences that build buinesses. These experiences live at the convergence of creative, media, data, and technology.

FIGURE I.1 The Razorfish Model

For us, Cisco and MLB were bright spots in the overall gloom that had fallen over the Internet business world in 2001 and 2002. They were hints of a convergence that would only pick up speed in years to come, as Amazon, Microsoft, and Apple continued to innovate, and Google, Facebook, and Twitter came on the scene. The lesson was that even in times of irrational exuberance, of high-flying IPOs, you might be skeptical that all is just media hype and little or nothing of long-lasting value is being created. You might even have that feeling now, what with Facebook's billion-dollar acquisition of the zero-revenue Instagram and the less-than-scintillating social media IPOs of 2012 fresh in your mind. The truth is that even most overinflated bubble produces long-lasting value. For all its flaws, the first dot-com bubble gave us eBay, Amazon, and, we humbly submit, Razorfish, a new type of consulting partner.

That 200-person company near death in 2002, whose brand was being written off by its new owners, is now more than 3,000 employees strong, with 20 offices all over the globe, and a central part of the fast-growing digital operation at our parent company, Publicis Groupe. Our client list runs from automakers like Ford Motor Co. and Mercedes-Benz, to packaged goods marketers like Kraft and Kellogg, to tech players like Microsoft and Samsung, to other blue chip companies like Unilever, UNIQLO, Staples, Nike, and Best Buy. Our success at creating both marketing experiences and technology solutions and products has led to recognition from numerous industry publications such as *Advertising Age*, who named us an A-List agency in both 2011 and 2012, and analysts like Gartner and Forrester, the latter of which called us a business transformer in their 2012 New Interactive Agency Landscape report.

We've made it because for more than 15 years we've lived at the center of the convergence and we've done it despite people telling us it couldn't be done.

For more information on the concepts explored in *Converge*, to connect with the authors, and for additional information on cited sources, visit convergebook.com.

Converge = Marketing + Technology

1 The Collision of Media, Technology, and Creativity

What is convergence? A little disambiguation, to borrow a term from Wikipedia, is in order. As a quick glance at that community-built encyclopedia will tell you, the concept of convergence holds meaning in fields from computer sciences and telecommunications, to economics, accounting, and sociology, to biology, mathematics, and logic. Convergence serves as the name of a Goth festival, an information technology (IT) show in the Philippines, and a Mexican political party. It's served as the title for several works of literature and music. Convergence, it's clear, means a lot of things to a lot of people. Its popularity reflects the era we live in, an epoch in which boundaries are made to be destroyed, in which unfamiliar ideas are brought together.

> Today, more than ever, the traditional boundaries between politics, culture, technology, finance, national security, and ecology are disappearing.
>
> —Thomas Friedman

There are strong forces at work here. The Internet has made communications cheap, instantaneous, and global. Inexpensive airfare and shifting international labor markets have uprooted millions, leaving them to bring their cultures and practices to new places, forging new, hybrid cultures. As *New York Times* columnist Thomas Friedman wrote years ago, "Today, more than

> The world feels smaller, yet it's no less complex.

ever, the traditional boundaries between politics, culture, technology, finance, national security, and ecology are disappearing." Friedman's point was that technological advances, chief among them the growth of the Internet, had globalized the world in a way that companies and nations had yet to understand. Boundaries between countries, once rigid and unyielding, had become permeable if not frail. The world feels smaller, yet it's no less complex.

Within the business world, competition isn't as clear-cut as it once was. Rivals once easily identified now appear as "frenemies," both adversary and collaborator. Friends like Google and Apple go to war overnight. A similar dynamic has occurred within individual businesses, even as they try to fight against it. It plays out in a lot of ways, but nowhere are the stakes higher than in how consumer experiences are created. This is where convergence comes in.

What we mean by convergence is the coming together of three irresistible forces—media, technology, and creativity—to meet an immovable object: the enterprise (Figure 1.1). We're only at the beginning of understanding these dynamics, but we do know one

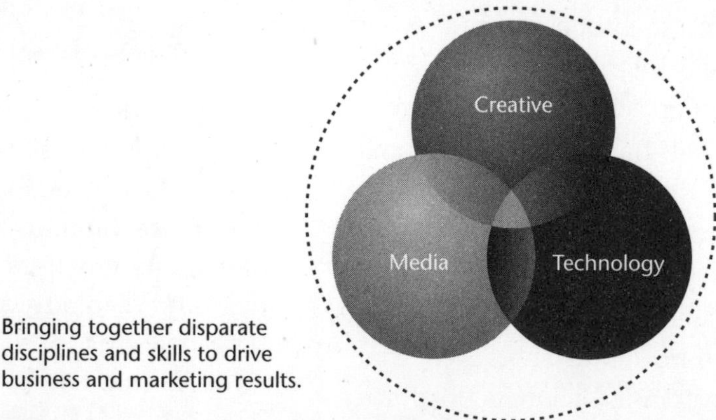

FIGURE 1.1 Convergence in Marketing

thing: Businesses have to change themselves quickly and dramatically if they want to survive and thrive. They need to rethink how they communicate with customers, the experiences they create, and how they're set up. The key, as we'll explain throughout this book, is to fully recognize the collision that's occurred and remake the company to deal with it.

The villain throughout this book is the silo. In ordinary parlance, a silo is a structure that contains a single item, usually grain. In business, writes David Aaker in *Spanning Silos,* a silo is "a metaphor for organizational units that contain their own management team and talent and lack the motivation or desire to work with or even communicate with other organizational units." He wrote, "Spanning silos, in my view, is the marketing challenge of our time." That was in 2008.

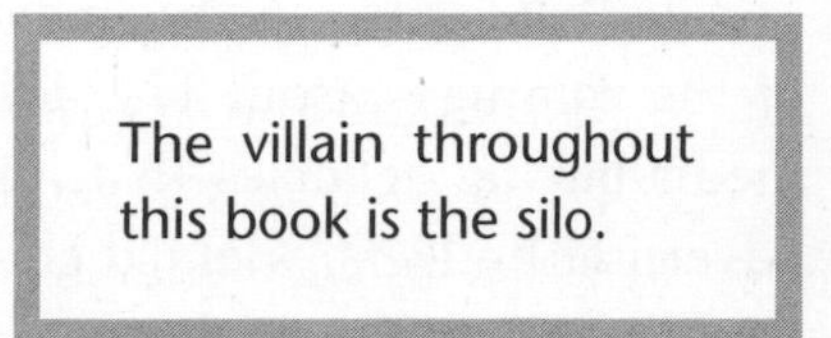

In the subsequent five years, the challenge is the same but the details have changed. Aaker was mainly concerned with how country and product silos hurt a business's attempts to efficiently create consistent marketing around the world. We'll take this in a different direction by focusing on how functional silos that separate tech from creativity and creativity from media are preventing brands from providing product and marketing experiences that consumers want and need. Aaker was concerned about the failure of integrated marketing communications, that is, programs that yoke together the various marketing disciplines in a unified way. We're concerned with a grander kind of integration that combines persuasive brand storytelling with powerful technology channels. We're focused on turning marketing itself into a product and service that customers need and want, the very thing that silos deny.

For decades, businesses could quite easily compartmentalize themselves as they tackled the challenges presented by media, technology, and creativity.

Let's look at how each discipline was handled in the traditional schema compared it to how it exists now.

Media

THEN: For decades there were two flavors of media: bought and earned. Paid media was something that could be bought every year in a showy event called the television upfront, when the TV networks put together a splashy party to roll out their new shows and get buyers to commit billions of their clients' ad dollars ahead of the coming season. The deal making was handled by specialist media-buying agencies that, through the aggregation of many big advertiser budgets, wielded great clout in the marketplace and thus could command scale discounts. Earned media, on the other hand, was attention won through public relations (PR) strategies that persuaded news reporters to write favorable articles about a company and its products.

NOW: The one-way communications model that used TV ads and PR to persuade consumers to buy your product is dead. Each consumer is a small, independent media company capable of publishing in multiple channels. The reputation of your brand rests on the whims of consumers. The communications landscape is reinvented every few months and, as a result, that glacial upfront process in which media is bought many months in advance makes little sense. PR agencies and departments struggle to organize around a communications ecosystem in which the consumer voice has been unboxed and amplified.

Technology

THEN: Technology was the back-end world of servers and intranets, traditionally the domain of the chief information officer (CIO) and the chief technology officer (CTO), each with very different responsibilities. Considered mere infrastructure, technology was noticeable mainly when it wasn't working and was more associated with the cost of doing business than innovation. Offshore systems integrators were hired to handle large-scale technology operations. IT organizations built and protected large-scale production and online systems such as travel-booking inventory managment, financial transactions, and manufacturing products.

NOW: No longer just a cost, with the right mind-set, technology can be a source of innovation that can lead to better products and better marketing. Data, application programming interfaces (APIs), and cloud computing are not just back-end concerns, but affect how brands are built and communicated. Technology helps identify better customer segments and optimize the stories that those customer segments are told. The chief marketing officer (CMO) and CTO now have new tools that were not available in the past to get their jobs done.

Creativity

THEN: Marketing communications were planned and executed through top-down processes. Highly paid art directors and writers fashioned themselves as the sole repository of creativity. Technology or media played a role in this process as distribution channels for ideas created on Madison Avenue. Go watch a few episodes of *Mad Men* to see how it was done.

NOW: Creativity is no longer the exclusive province of marketing and creative departments. Great ideas might come from crowdsourced creative platforms like Victors & Spoils, from an iOS developer, or from your consumer, who is using social media to give you an easily accessed, always-on suggestion box for your product or brand. Technology and media don't just disseminate creative ideas, they inform them.

For a long time, perhaps until the beginning part of this decade, it was easy enough to think of media, creativity, and technology as three distinct biomes. The CMO didn't need to be conversant with server technology. The CIO wasn't concerned with marketing. And marketing agencies didn't need to be concerned with the technology that supported its advertising ideas or the media budgets that disseminated them. There was a very linear chain, from planning and strategy, to creative brainstorming, execution, and production, to distribution through the media, whether bought (ads) or earned (PR).

All that has changed because the consumer has changed.

Sony Ericsson predicts that there will be more than 3 billion smartphone subscriptions by 2017, increasing data traffic to 15 times what it is today. That means a little less than half the world will be walking around with a level of computing in their pocket that would have been unthinkable just 15 years ago. Meanwhile, continual improvements in software development make all of this computing power easier for people to use.

Now consider the plights of those once easily organized silos. Technology is media. Media is creativity. Jumble it up any way you want. Like the famous Möbius strip, you can't tell what's what anymore. The only thing that matters is the quality of the consumer experience. Companies more and more are realizing that your consumer experience is the strongest reflection of your brand.

Consider these real-world examples:

- Convergence has changed how people browse and shop, and smart brands are responding by creating an omnichannel experience. Tesco Homeplus, the South Korean operation of the U.K.-based grocer Tesco, created a virtual store in subways, where images of food were projected on walls and laid out like actual stores. Each item had a quick response (QR) code so commuters/shoppers could use their smartphones to scan the item and have it delivered right as they got home. The program gave Tesco Homeplus the lead in online sales, which grew 130 percent and helped close the gap offline with market leader E-Mart, despite not having as many stores. And if you're thinking that won't scale or won't work in the United States and other countries where the wireless infrastructure isn't as good, try this: The online grocer Peapod, after successful pilots in Philadelphia and Chicago, recently announced plans to open 100 virtual stores in Boston, New York City, Washington, DC, and other locales.

FIGURE 1.2 Tesco Homeplus Putting the Customer Front and Center

Tesco Homeplus made it easy for folks at train stations to restock their fridge from their cell phones.

- Brand stories are now told in a way that takes advantage of popular social platforms. A movement toward open APIs gives third-party developer communities the opportunity to layer all kinds of innovation onto existing platforms and is changing the face of marketing and commerce. American Express has worked with Twitter, Facebook, Foursquare, Zynga, and other digital giants as it builds out its concept of social currency, a kind of social-media-age twist on its loyalty programs that links merchants and consumers through social media. Meanwhile, Nike has released the API for the Nike+ FuelBand, its personal fitness device, allowing developers to add NikeFuel features to other platforms (Figure 1.3).
- Much like APIs, data is playing a greater role in how companies fine-tune their targeting and storytelling strategies. Target offered a classic example in 2012, when it became known that the retailer was aware that a teen girl was pregnant before her

FIGURE 1.3 NikeFuel Inspiring a New Generation of Quantified Selves

Nike's FuelBand and company-native applications make it easy for folks to monitor and track being fit.

> family was. By sifting through customer-buying habits, a Target data scientist was able to find correlations between women who bought large amounts of lotion or supplements and those who ended up on the baby registry. Thanks to that way of thinking, the company is able to get to mothers early in their pregnancy and win them over with coupons.

Although these examples span the world and the business community, there is a common thread running through them. They are technologically enabled experiences that create value for consumers. Whether saving time in the case of Tesco Homeplus, money in the case of American Express, or health in the case of Nike, they are far from the world where marketing is interruption. And they are just as far from a world where marketing is just cost.

To put yourself in a position to create these kinds of experiences, you have to reject some timeworn ideas and practices that put marketing in one part of the operation and technology and media in another. You have to bring all three together in a way that makes sense for the consumer. Put simply, you have to embrace convergences and reject silos. This is delicate business because, in deconstructing these silos, you're challenging the status quo that has made companies successful for many decades.

Building the Renaissance Organization

Think back just five or six years. How many of the products and concepts that are part of our world today weren't even around? As recently as 2007, there were very few popular phones with global positioning systems (GPS). There was no App Store, no Instagram, Pinterest, Foursquare, or Spotify. Facebook had a paltry (for them) 70 million users. You couldn't buy a phone with Android on it. Today, Facebook has celebrated its billionth customer, more than 10 billion Apple apps have been downloaded, and Android is the most popular mobile operating system by market share. It's mind-blowing how far we've come in such a short period.

Yet that pace of change we feel as consumers is rarely mirrored in businesses that serve up the experiences. Much of this has to do with how large companies are organized. Generally, businesses are still stuck in organization silos, with archaic incentive plans tied to rigid profit-and-loss (P&L) centers. And within P&L silos there are departmental silos. We freely admit that we even struggle with this at Razorfish, with all of our global regions and practice areas.

Of course, it doesn't have to be this way. The most valuable company in history is Apple. Guess how many profit and loss centers it has? One. To match its straightforward product and pricing approaches, Apple has an extremely simple organizational chart that has, as *Fortune* writer Adam Lashinsky put it, "none of the dotted-line or matrixed responsibilities popular elsewhere in the corporate world." Only the chief financial office (CFO) has a P&L. As Lashinsky writes, "It's a radical example of Apple's different course: Most companies view the P&L as the ultimate proof of a manager's accountability; Apple turns that dictum on its head by labeling P&L a distraction that only the finance chief needs to consider. The result is a command-and-control structure where ideas are shared at the top—if not below."

Another result of that way of doing business is a seamless experience for the consumer as he or she travels from the website to a physical store. Select your new Mac online and pick it up at the store. Don't like the new iPad that you bought on Apple.com? Then you can either ship it back or take it to the nearest store. Apple doesn't care, unlike many retailers who will only accept in-store returns at the location where the item was purchased. Chances are that many of those companies have their physical stores reporting up through a different P&L than does the online store. The respective business leaders aren't incentivized to work together to create that reliable, uniform experience across the points where consumers interact with the brand. In the world of omnichannel commerce that we'll examine later, where the customer can make purchases from more and more touchpoints, these businesses are setting themselves up to fail.

The problem is that too many companies are essentially showing their organizational chart to consumers. They're letting their back-end organizational biases shape how consumers interact with their brand, rather than the other way around. This is why startups can be so effective in disrupting existing businesses. Their success is typically a result of an orientation that begins with the consumer and her wants and needs. Everyone at the startup is marshaling toward that. There is no org chart to get in the way of consumer experience and the associated journey.

We just offered Apple as an example of an enterprise whose success to some degree hinges on a lack of P&Ls that inspire fiefdoms and self-interest rather than cooperation and collaboration. Now we'll use Apple as an example of what you shouldn't do.

Take a look at Apple.com. As part of a minimal, functional design that leads the way easily to its products, you'll see photographs of its products, maybe some video. You might think those images are chosen or approved by the executive who oversees the online store. Nope. Throughout the company, images are the bailiwick of the graphics arts department. When Ron Johnson was retail chief, he had no say over inventory. That was then–chief operations officer, and now-CEO, Tim Cook's department. "Specialization," writes *Fortune*'s Lashinsky, "is the norm at Apple, and as a result, Apple employees aren't exposed to functions outside their area of expertise."

We'd respectfully submit that for the many, many companies that aren't Apple this sort of functional ghettoization is no better than creating several competing P&Ls and is still probably the wrong way to do business. Apple can get away with it because it's achieved a best-in-class status and, for a long time at least, it had a visionary, one-of-a-kind business leader making top-down decisions on all parts of the business. This, as we're sure you'll agree, is not business as usual. Your company is probably not helmed by a consumer and product visionary with insight into every bit of your product and marketing experience. Your CEO probably doesn't want weekly meetings with the ad team. Nor does the CEO want to change the price of a major new product at the last minute.

This is why the Apple approach likely won't work for you.

Every organization needs specialists and experts, but in the place of environments where everyone fills one role and thinks about nothing besides that role, there needs to be cross-fertilization, a coming together of various fields, disciplines, personalities, and cultures. *The Medici Effect,* a 2006 book by Frans Johansson, catalogs success stories where just this sort of cross-fertilization happens. He writes, "When you step into an intersection of fields, disciplines, or cultures, you can combine existing concepts into a large number of extraordinary new ideas."

His examples are culled from cooking, the arts, and even the business world. He tells of Corning's history of innovating in glass that touches everything from Edison's lightbulb to casserole dishes that won't crack when you move them from the freezer straight to the oven. The head of the glass research group considers her main responsibility to get the right person for the right job, so she maintains a creativity room where people can talk about whatever they want. One time, she invited a theoretical physicist working quietly on quantum mechanics to join an actual product team. His work, Johansson writes, "suddenly was able to have a greater impact on Corning's bottom line than anything he had done in the past eight years."

The key is to remove what he calls "associative barriers" that block us from finding intersections where creativity happens. Johansson again: "A person with high associative barriers will quickly arrive at conclusions when confronted with a problem since their thinking is more focused. He or she will recall how the problem has been handled in the past, or how others in similar situations solved it. A person with low associative barriers, on the other hand, may think to connect ideas or concepts that have very little basis in past experience, or that cannot easily be traced logically."

Removing associative barriers by exposing yourself to other cultures ("tech, meet marketing; marketing, meet tech!") and reversing assumptions, will take you to those intersections where creativity happens. This is a wonderful model for the world in which we live and it's one that brands and their partners have to get used to.

The problem is that enterprises, in well-meaning but ultimately misguided bids for efficiency, organizational simplicity, and accountability, have erected and maintained some of the highest associative barriers you'd ever want to see. These barriers are the silos that quash collaboration and cocreation, ensure fiefdoms, and cause delays and discord.

The Five Principles of Convergence

Throughout this book, we'll look at many ways in which successful brands are using technology to create brilliant experiences for their customers. Although the brands will vary wildly in category, size, culture, and age, ranging from icons like Mercedes-Benz to relative newbies like Moosejaw Mountaineering, a thorough look under the hoods will reveal that they all stay true to a set of principles that have set them up for success in the digital age. We call these the five principles of Convergence.

The first principle is customer centricity. Here the company is not beholden to some age-old organizational chart but structured around the customer journey, with individual accountability for each part of that journey. Strategy is based on data from actual consumer activity, not abstract gut feeling. And that data dictates not only what experiences are served but where, when, and how. Customer-centric brand communications engage the consumer in social ecosystems and through open APIs, and customer-centric retail experience is omnichannel, giving consumers the same experience whether they're in-store, online, or on the phone.

The second principle is the rejection of silos. Realizing that marketing, technology, and creativity are no longer discrete problems, converged enterprises are working toward enabling better collaboration among functions. Technology is no longer a support function. Marketing is no longer just about campaigns. The organization has senior roles like chief digital officer and chief marketing technologists, filled by experts who catalyze innovation throughout the organization and foster collaboration. Internal account management is used so that marketing people have clear lines of communication with tech and vice versa.

This brings us to our third principle. Companies taking advantage of convergence act like start-ups. That doesn't mean free sushi lunches for all employees or ping-pong tables or other Silicon Valley window dressing. Instead, it's an approach to technology and organizational structure. Enterprise deploys—or at least experiments with—cheap, fast, and flexible tools like cloud computing, social media platforms, and open APIs. There are product managers who are accountable for particular aspects of the consumer experience, just like Facebook has tasked someone with oversight of its newsfeed. This outlook is vital to creating brand experiences that engage customers over the long term. These organizations employ Agile methodology, rapid prototype new products, and services.

The fourth principle is a cross-disciplinary mind-set. As described above, this is about looking for intersections where innovation can occur and removing associative barriers. The trick is to get a wide variety of expertise around the table and incentivize collaboration among functions and disciplines.

The fifth principle is to think of your brand as a service. For many companies, this presents a mind-set/culture change. You're no longer in the business of selling stuff; you're filling customers' needs. You're creating an always-on ecosystem, not just a series of campaigns based around a calendar of product launches. Nike is the classic example with its ecosystem of fitness apparel, gadgets like FuelBand and services like Nike+ that immerse the user in Nike innovation and create an end-to-end fitness solution. In evolutionary terms this makes the old line of trainers that could be marketed with a slogan and a celebrity ad campaign look like a knuckle-dragging caveman.

While no company has mastered all of these principles, any company that's now succeeding has adopted at least a few of them. As we move through the book, you'll see how these principles are the bedrock of innovation in our age.

Convergence Catalysts

- Identify and break down silos, the enterprise version of associative barriers. Map your organization to the consumer experience with individual accountability for each part of the customer journey.
- Use product managers, not marketing managers. It's no longer about throwing a message out into the world and hoping that you interrupt the right person at the right time. Marketing has become about service, about utility, and much of it is technology enabled.

- Inspire cross-disciplinary thinking. Just as Corning realized the egghead sitting quietly in the corner could bring insight to the creation of new glass products, you too need to embrace diversity of all forms in your organization.
- Insist on collaboration, both within and outside the organization. The future is about partnerships. Ask yourself, how are you working with social and mobile platforms, with media companies, with your own consumers and could you improve?
- Make time to understand technology. While you don't need to learn how to write code, you do need to understand the limits of the technologies you're using and dive deep into technologies you're not using, especially around the cloud and data.

Oh, and there's one more item to put on your to-do list. Last but far from least, you have to understand the figure at the center of it all: the consumer.

2 Next-Generation Storytelling

In fall 2012, Microsoft launched Windows 8, a radical makeover of the company's operating system (OS) designed for an increasingly multiscreen world. Its slick, colorful, tile-based interface that works so well on touchscreens generated a lot of fanfare, as did the effort to make an OS that created a consistent experience across a desktop or notebook computer, a mobile phone, and a tablet.

A less frequently told part of the Windows 8 story was Microsoft's efforts to bring advertisers into the fold early on and get them thinking about how brands could be integrated into the slate of apps to be embedded inside the operating system. At launch there were five such ads ready to go. Pepperidge Farm slipped an ad for Goldfish crackers into a Slacker Radio app; Chrysler's Jeep ad went into My AccuWeather. The takeaway lessons for large enterprises is that unless you are part of these platform releases, you won't get the lessons of how to adapt to new platforms. When you consider that Microsoft's desktop platform still drives over 80 percent of the earth's computers, building on new versions of this platform has to be mission critical.[1]

[1]http://en.wikipedia.org/wiki/Usage_share_of_operating_systems

We submit that what we just described to you is a microcosm of the future of creativity. The next generation of storytelling is about expressing brands through technology. This is the key to inspiring and engaging consumers and getting them to help you tell your brand story. As Frank Rose wrote in *The Art of Immersion,* "People have always wanted to in some way inhabit the stories that move them. The only variable is whether technology gives them that opportunity."

It follows that if you don't understand technology, it's going to be very difficult for you to figure out how a brand is going to express itself in the future. Someone who understands a Windows or iOS platform can express a brand very differently than an executive creative director who cut their teeth during the television era.

In a way, the major computing platforms, whether desktop or mobile OSs, social networks, or video game consoles, are the new TV—at least in terms of the numbers of consumers they reach and the amount of time we spend with them. Windows 7, for instance, sold more than 700 million licenses. Through March of 2012, more than 365 million iOS devices had been sold. Facebook has more than 1 billion users; Twitter, more than a half-billion. Very few TV programs reach even one-tenth of that audience. We admit that comparing TV to digital platforms is like comparing apples to oranges; we're not advocating that anyone surrender their media plan to only in-app advertising. The overarching point is that a lot of people spend a lot of time on these platforms, much as they have done with TV throughout the decades.

But working with platforms isn't as straightforward as working with TV. It requires different orientations and processes, muscles, talent, and skill sets. For the most part, TV is a static medium. Although TV screens get bigger and better and programming trends change, the process of buying and producing ads doesn't. The 30-second spot still reigns supreme despite the rise of digital video recorders that many thought would reduce skippable ads to an afterthought. Outside of production techniques, there's very little technological or technical expertise that goes along with developing and airing a TV spot. You buy the media, hire an agency, concept the spot, hire a production company, and produce the spot and air it. Voilà. Rinse and repeat. You're simply dropping your ad into a system whose rules and logic are well known.

Not so for platforms.

Platforms change so often that they might as well be regarded as living, breathing things. That's why they're often referred to as ecosystems. Like any kind of ecosystem, the platform is affected by a host of internal and external factors, from new versions and upgrades to the work of consumers and third-party developers. Because they're moving targets, understanding platforms requires deep technological partnerships. Designing branded experiences for platforms is more akin to designing software than it is making TV ads. You don't have to cozy up to the folks at NBC or MTV to get a new ad on the air. In contrast, it certainly helps if you've got a good relationship with Microsoft or Apple or any of the other major platform players so that they can let you in early on development and help you understand what the next iteration of the platform is going to look like and how it's going to behave.

Next-generation storytelling is about three major trends, all of which can be seen in that example: the democratization of creativity, rise of collaboration, and reimagining of brands as services. Each of these on its own is a powerful force for change; taken together they're reshaping the creative process in marketing organizations and ad agencies. To understand how, we'll look at each of these trends in depth. But first we need to take a step back and look at how this creative process has emerged over time.

The Death of the Mad Man and the Birth of the Creative Technologist

The current popular notion of how the ad agency creative process comes down through *Mad Men,* the heavily awarded drama about the triumphs and travails of a 1960s New York ad agency. Its protagonist, Don Draper, is a child of the Great Depression and a veteran of the Korean War who has come to some prominence as a creative thinker during the first creative revolution in advertising, when Bill Bernbach came up with "Lemon" and "Think Small" to help turn around the Volkswagen brand.

For Draper, the creative process goes something like this: Roll into the office with a nasty hangover, have some coffee and maybe a doughnut, take a nap on the couch in his office, have a meeting and bark at some junior staffer, have a meeting and storm out on a client, take a multiple-whiskey lunch, another nap, do some more barking, some more drinking, some more napping, and he's out the door at 5 PM.

Although this is most definitely an exaggerated portrayal, it does bear a relation to how the ad agency business had understood creativity for much of its existence. For decades, the ad creative was a cousin to the amateur filmmaker who writes, directs, and maybe even stars in his own movie, exerting maximum creative control and producing films that are the expression of a single creative mind. From the mid-century to the 1990s, senior creative directors, the real-life counterparts of Don Draper, exerted a similar degree of god-like control. Their creative vision was the result of a long planning cycle, closed-door brainstorming process, and expensive production outlays, and it was supported by massive investments in paid media, especially television. It's no accident that the broadcast category at Cannes Lions awards—the Oscars of the ad industry—is known as film. Creative directors, often frustrated novelists and screenwriters, were trying to create art that happened to sell stuff.

All that has changed. Although big-budget TV commercials are still important to certain kinds of brands, they're only a portion of today's marketing activity. Enlightened organizations understand that the hallmarks of the TV age need to be rethought, if not demolished. So where was once a single vision, there is collaboration. Where there was feedback or iterations, there is cocreation. Where there was once a creative, there is a creative technologist.

Technology is in no small way responsible for this, even though it took some time to figure things out.

The early days of digital marketing—the awkward-in-retrospect era of pop-ups and banners—tried to simply shoehorn traditional advertising ideas into a handful of ad formats cooked up for the Internet. These were the days of integrated marketing communications, the industry's initial attempt to make sense of a rapidly increasing number of consumer touchpoints. For years, there was just TV, radio, print, and out-of-home. The growth of digital marketing and few other developments, such as digital video recorders (DVRs), called into question the viability of the TV ad and began to complicate things. At first anyway, the ad business dealt with the Internet as just another force leading to audience fragmentation, lumping it in with proliferation of cable channels. Possible alternatives to dealing with this fragmentation included public relations (PR) and direct marketing, disciplines once venerable and dismissed as "below the line" that were suddenly brought to the strategic table. And there were some new solutions such as viral, buzz, guerilla, and word-of-mouth marketing. In short, there were now many buckets into which a big advertising idea would be slopped, a reality that gave rise to concepts like 360-degree marketing and the like.

The past few years have seen the repudiation of that way of box-checking thinking thanks to a central realization that "digital" or "online" is not a box, but something much bigger and more foundational. The shift is from one unique big-brand message that's packed up into a set of "matching luggage" to multiple ideas for multiple audiences based on a single coherent brand platform. Digital is not a bucket to be filled or a bag to be packed; it is an enabler of experiences. Nor is digital purely a set of tools that are inherited by marketers. These days, if you're savvy enough and have the right relationships and technological talent, you can impact the creation of the tools and the development platforms themselves. Managing this shift, which impacts all parties to the marketing world, requires a set of talents and skills that are very un-Draperesque.

Consider:

- Consumers are no longer passive receptacles for marketing ideas. Increasingly, they are helping to cocreate the marketing idea and amplify the messaging through social channels and gamification. The flip side is that they will shoot your idea down if it doesn't pass the BS test.
- Brands become services. It's no longer about manipulating consumers into buying products. The question becomes the following: How can my brand help the consumer achieve a goal? Marketing becomes less spin and more about authenticity and utility. Brands also become sources of data.
- Media is a combination of paid, earned, and owned, and the lines between them are increasingly very blurry. Storytelling is often concurrent rather than sequential.
- Creative agencies must overcome their fear of data and use it to inform the experiences they build for consumers. It's about art + science, not just art and not just science.

The result of all these changes is a recalibration of a very central marketing formula.

In the old days, this is what it looked like:

Planning Insights + Ad Agency Creativity = A New Ad

Now it's something like this, an equation in which technology is an essential part of creativity:

Native Data + Open API + Collaborative Creativity = New Brand Experiences

This shift raises a lot of questions around the role of the lead agency, a discussion that's framed in many different ways. Should digital agencies now own the title of lead agency? Or maybe PR shops should, since earned media has become so important? Maybe we need media-agnostic, execution-neutral communications planners to keep the foxes out of the henhouse? And these lines of

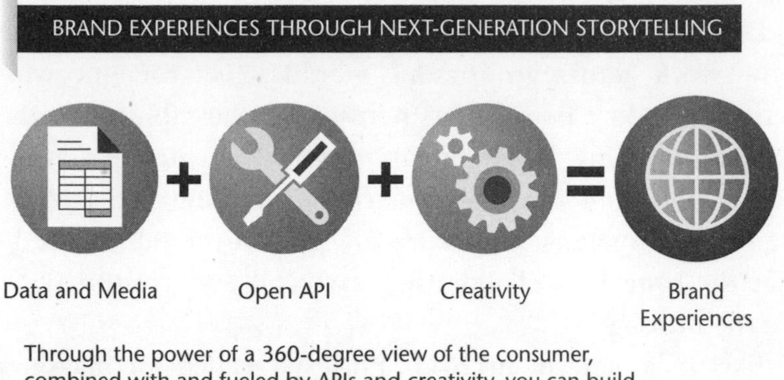

Through the power of a 360-degree view of the consumer, combined with and fueled by APIs and creativity, you can build powerful digital experiences on any platform.

FIGURE 2.1 Storytelling Requires Technology for Effective Communication

questioning have led to constant self-examination on the part of all kinds of ad agencies as they struggle to find just the right structures, processes, and positioning to situate themselves as a lead agency.

We think this is wrongheaded.

No one agency can do it all anymore, and even if we did, we'd be wrong. For years now, all signs have pointed to a reality where clients prefer relatively large agency rosters that provide them with best-in-class services—this, despite the best attempts of ad agencies to offer all-in-one solutions that would give clients soup to nuts. This was a good effort, but one that was bound to come up short in a digital world. There is simply too much complexity, too great a call for specialization, and too much expertise needed in too many areas to assume that a single company could contain it all.

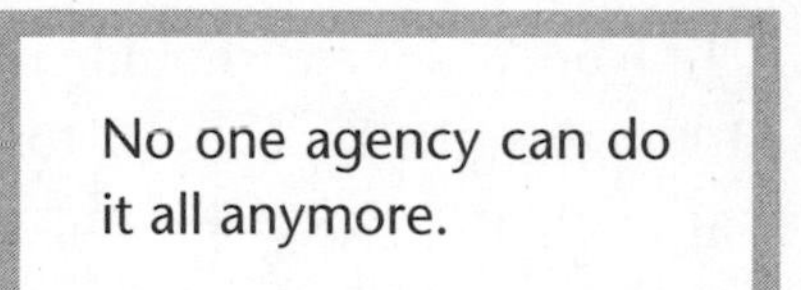

Brands need creative partners, user experience partners, technology partners, mobile partners, and social partners, to name just a few. The universe of customer touchpoints is exponentially growing. The agency can no longer operate as a gatekeeper, fending off other potential collaborators. The way for the client to win is for him or her to open up the structure. This is exactly what some of our most forward-looking clients do. They understand they need to assemble a diverse team, sometimes breaking up the work across groups one would never imagine working together. The key is to bring them all to the table through new processes enabling better collaboration. It typically starts with an all-agency and technology-partner planning meeting, where upcoming campaigns, and briefs are put on the table. The key is to set the tone for collaboration early on and continually reinforce the message.

Others have agreed. In 2011, Forrester called for marketers to dump the lead agency model. "Campaign planning that starts with the 30-second ad and tries to force-fit it to the Web blunts interactive possibilities," the report states. "The time has come for a clean slate." It should be replaced with a structure that's "more open and flexible and that allows each discipline greater freedom to express the campaign strategy."

In reality, this has already started to happen. The marketplace has been issuing calls for open-source agency models for at least five years, when it became clear that the consumer and media landscape had become too complex for any one agency to own. The rise of mobile and social has only amplified that need.

But open source shouldn't be assumed to mean structure-free. Although some are content to do jump balls for major assignments, many clients, especially big marketers with varied brand portfolios, demonstrate the need for hierarchies. Procter & Gamble, by way of example, used what it calls the brand agency leader model, establishing a single point of contact for each of its brands who then act as general contractors changed with hiring other agencies and partners as needed. The leader isn't expected to do all the work but rather to find potential collaborators. Some marketers have turned to agency holding companies to establish dedicated cross-functional teams, but not even the holding company boundaries are sacrosanct anymore. In 2011, Chevrolet demanded that rivals Interpublic and Omnicom form a joint venture called Commonwealth for its new agency.

The lead agency has been replaced by the lead client, often contorting his or her partners to get maximum value out of them. And the chief creative officer has become chief curator in role if not in title. We have to wonder what Don Draper and his friends at the agency would think of this.

He'd probably have a drink.

The Democratization of Creativity

In September of 2011, Google and Apple made interesting announcements about the state of their app stores. Apple went first, announcing there were currently 700,000 applications available worldwide. Google then countered with its own figure: 675,000 were available in its store. For Apple, there have been more downloads of apps than music (reported by ASYMCO on July 13, 2011). These are stunning figures, when you consider that both app stores were only about four years old. That growth is what happens when you don't limit creativity and innovation to the walls of your own company and give people tools that they can use to make things, possibly the greatest enabler of the changes we discussed in the previous section.

For decades now, the playing field for anyone who wants to make stuff has gotten more and more level. In the 1980s, Apple introduced desktop publishing. Then HTML made it so that anyone could publish a Web page, and a host of companies from Six Apart to WordPress to Tumblr made it even easier to have your say online. iMovie and Quicktime made video editing easier, just as GarageBand made it possible to create your own tunes from your bedroom. Then came the social networks to help you distribute it all. And then there's the frenetic world of mobile development. With Xcode, Eclipse, and Visual Studio, making apps for the iPhone, iPad, Android, or Microsoft Windows 8 is approachable for anyone.

The result has been an explosion of creativity around the world.

One of the best ways to see how this history has unfolded is through the story of Adobe. In November of 2012, we chatted with Shantanu Narayen, CEO of Adobe and longtime vet of the technology world. After starting his early career at Apple and Silicon Graphics, he cofounded a photo-sharing service. He then went on to join Adobe, rising to his current post in 2007. In 2011, he was named to President Obama's Management Advisory Board. Narayen is well situated to understand the changes wracking the marketing world today.

As he sees it, there are three megatrends affecting the creative process: the move to the cloud, the rise of mobile devices, and social media.

"There is more change in creative now with the confluence of these three megatrends than at any time in my career," he said. "Technology has enabled everyone to be a publisher and has democratized creative in a way that's never happened before. People want consistent experiences across multiple screens and expect their content everywhere."

Adobe's role in these trends is unique because it's both influencing the game and responding to it. After its founding in the early 1980s, Adobe released a slate of important products that changed the face of advertising, publishing, and other industries. There was Illustrator, the drawing program released in 1986, which influenced the world of graphic design. A couple of years later Adobe's flagship Photoshop arrived on the scene, introducing photo and graphics editing to the masses. In the 1990s it purchased PageMaker; it later released InDesign, transforming page layout, and also created the ubiquitous Portable Document Format (PDF). These would all be wrapped together into a product called the Creative Suite, a bundle of applications that would grow to include all the tools needed for graphic design, video editing, and Web design. This has become a mainstay of creative departments, but Adobe didn't stop there.

Seeing the increased spending going into digital marketing and understanding the growing need for a better quantitative understanding of what creative is working and what isn't, Adobe bet big on data and bought Omniture in 2009. The well-known Omniture was the leading Web analytics company, with a cloud infrastructure that in 2012 processed 6 trillion transactions. Its acquisition gave Adobe a huge window into Web analytics, crucial for marketers to understand just how successful their creations were at attracting and engaging audiences.

In 2010, Adobe made another move to enable the promise of analytics and content with the purchase of the Day CQ enterprise content management system. Now Adobe has connected content creation and analytics in a way that can be dynamically served up. With the proliferation of microsegmentations driven by machine learning, marketers need a dynamic content engine and Adobe Experience Manager is that engine.

Building on content and analytics, in 2011, Adobe acquired Efficient Frontier, now known as Adobe AdLens, a management system that uses real-time analysis and mathematical models to help marketers decide how to allocate their online advertising media spend across search, display, and social to maximize return on investment (ROI). This gave Adobe the added dimension of automation for marketing decision making.

Having acquired a critical mass of products targeting marketers, Adobe launched the Adobe Marketing Cloud, an integrated set of technology solutions that help marketers understand and manage the impact of their activity. Here's how Narayen described it: "If you use social or content or media analytics, you can have a single, unified dashboard to look at a customer profile or a campaign or a particular budget and understand its impact."

Adobe's move into data is a response to increased pressure on agencies and brands to demonstrate results. Put simply, there is more accountability these days in the marketing world. Not even Adobe, with its creative orientation, could ignore that.

"Measuring efficiency of marketing spend, effectiveness of brand campaigns and new websites has become far more standard," Narayen said. "In the past, you'd create a great website and if it was aesthetically pleasing—inherently subjective—you felt the task was accomplished."

Now it's all about quantifiable results.

The Marketing Cloud also puts Adobe in position to help its users manage the entire life cycle of a piece of content, from its creation through measurement, management, and monetization. This has changed Adobe's value to organizations as well. For a magazine publisher such as Condé Nast, Adobe products have long been a favorite for the production of its glossy magazines such as *Vogue*, *GQ*, or *The New Yorker*. Then, as digital has become more central to publishers, Adobe has stepped up its game, staying relevant with content management on websites and mobile devices, measuring and helping drive new business models.

"We've become far more mission critical," Narayen said. "Rather than just the creative community swearing by Adobe, now we're helping the customer's entire business."

That Adobe has found itself in this position is a proof point of how the world has changed. Narayen rattled off a few examples of where this is happening, including a big box retailer who is considering the deployment of a tablet app to replace circulars. As shoppers walk around the store, the app fills them in on product information and location.

"It's actually happening across all industries, because nobody's going to be spared the need to provide more relevant information," he said. "People who combine both creative and data will produce experiences that stand out above the noise now."

Collaboration: Chief Creative Becomes Chief Curator

Throughout its history, Axe, the body spray brand made and marketed by Unilever, has promoted its wares to young men through ads featuring attractive women. The proposition is simple as can be: Use Axe and a disproportionately good-looking lady will find you absolutely irresistible. Since the product's launch more than a decade ago, the approach has worked, with Axe taking nearly three-quarters of market share by some calculations.

When Axe added a body spray for women to its product line, called Anarchy, a different approach was called for. Some of this was handled by tweaking the TV commercials so that the attraction is less one-sided and more mutual—and by making the men better looking. But we also had to find a way to tell this story in digital channels. Enter Razorfish's role.

To take the brand to Axe's large online community and beyond, we created a digital graphic novel—and we use the phrase "we created" in only the loosest sense. We actually teamed up with Aspen Comics and Scott Lobdell, probably best known for his work on Marvel's *X-Men*. But not even they can take credit for the work created on behalf of Axe—much of that goes to the consumer.

Together, over a four-month period, we concocted—as far as we know—the first comic book written by and starring its readers. The crafting of the story all took place in public, in real time, with fans of the brand and the genre using social media to recommend plot points and character developments or to vote on others' plot and character suggestions. It was a reimagining of the graphic novel for a generation raised real time with the Web. Within two days of launch, the project was featured in dozens of publications and had garnered thousands of tweets. Over the long haul, there were more than 3 million views of the trailer and more than 1 million site views. Fifty thousand votes were cast and 15,000 suggestions were made. Axe engagement records were broken and Anarchy became the best-selling body spray in the United States, while Axe had the biggest increase in market share across an entire category.

What was so special about this campaign?

Most important, it illustrates how the creative process has changed in recent years to the collaborative process we mentioned earlier in this chapter. Within the Anarchy program, there are multiple layers of collaboration beyond the client-agency interaction, which we take as a given. First, there was the decision to work with Aspen, whose reputation in the comic book world precedes it. Its work includes a Web comic based on the NBC series *Heroes,* not to mention original works like—and this will be relevant to you senior executives out there—*Executive Assistant Assassins*. Aspen is also itself a well-known collaborator with industry giants DC and Marvel. Who better to handle the creation of a digital comic book than the experts? It was a move that gave the Anarchy project instant credibility.

The collaboration didn't stop there. Rather than have Aspen's writers and artists plot out the story from beginning to end, using Razorfish-provided brand cues, the creative process was opened up. Consumers got the ball rolling plot-wise and helped control the direction it took. Users could contribute ideas at the YouTube channel, the campaign's hub, or on Facebook or Twitter. Every few days, new chapters were added, so fans could in short order see the fruits of their interest—and some of those fans were even built into the story. Seeing the creative process evolve in real time kept interest levels high throughout the campaign, which is extremely important during a product launch.

Another Razorfish cocreation campaign was for McDonald's Germany, which wanted to make its fortieth anniversary a social happening. A promotional burger was the obvious step, but there'd been so many of those over the years that a little innovation was required to freshen it up. Working with Razorfish, they came up with the idea of doing the first crowdsourced burger, in which the consumer would invent the burger, vote for it, and then eat it.

We developed what was known as the Burger Configurator, a Web app that allowed fans to mix and match more than 70 ingredients and condiments to create the beefy concoctions of their liking. There was only a small media budget to promote the campaign, so we created a do-it-yourself marketing approach for the would-be burger chefs. Fans could create videos, banners, and posters to promote their burgers. The top five performers, among them pretzel bun burgers, an Italian-style chicken burger, and a curry- and chili-flavored sandwich with chorizo and jalapeños, were test marketed in German McDonald's locations. The winner got his own TV commercial.

The results were impressive:

- 7 million page impressions on the website
- 45,000 burger creations in the first seven days with no media budget spent
- 116,000 burger creations in total
- 12,000 people created their own marketing campaigns
- 1.5 million voters
- Reach that extended to one out of four online Germans

The central lesson from both the McDonald's and the Axe work is how a contemporary agency these days needs to understand its role in the creative process. The role for the executive creative director—or other very senior creatives—has become curation, not just idea generation, and collaboration.

> The role for the executive creative director—or other very senior creatives—has become curation, not just idea generation, and collaboration.

Collaboration and curation, although not the same, are intimately related in today's marketing and technology world. Both require the dismantling of egos and changing timeworn definitions of creativity.

Curation has taken on new importance in a world of too much information. Each one of us needs to find our filters, that is, the people or platforms that tell us what's worth consuming. To see good examples, look to the blog Boing Boing, or BrainPickings, the site run by Maria Popova that provides a stream of smart, well-chosen content about a variety of topics from art and literature to creativity and science. And increasingly, brands such as American Express, IBM, and Harley-Davidson are finding that they're able to fill the curator role, often with help from agencies or outside partners. A company worth examining from this point of view is Percolate, founded a few years ago by former digital strategist Noah Brier. Using a large amount of data and algorithms tied to a brand's areas of interest,

Percolate's software helps brands produce content at scale by recommending content worth sharing from millions of sources.

Collaboration is about assembling the right creative ideas for the right technological and media solutions and pulling together the right talent to get the job done in the most efficient and effective way for the client. For many creatives, this has become a tough pill to swallow. They got into the ad game thinking it would be an outlet for their creativity; instead, they're finding that it's often more a question of harnessing and synthesizing others' great ideas or building on preexisting platforms, with the understanding that the more places from which they source creative ideas, the greater the likelihood of success.

This is the fundamental principle of a small wave of crowdsourcing agencies that have caused some upset on Madison Avenue over the past few years. Crowdsourcing isn't limited to agencies. The idea actually came from the technology world, led by Richard Stallman, with open source–based software back in the 1960s. Modern-day examples include massive code and knowledge-sharing platforms such as GitHub, or even the crowdsourced development platforms such as topcoder.com. Agencies have tried to translate some of these ideas to the marketing services world. Perhaps the best known among them is Victors & Spoils. Founded by former Crispin Porter & Bogusky executives, Victors & Spoils gives its network of freelance creatives the opportunity to take a swing at briefs from some pretty big brands, such as Chipotle, Coca-Cola, Converse, General Mills, Harley-Davidson, Levi's, Virgin America, and, yes, Unilever. Costs are low because Victors & Spoils hasn't assumed all the overhead that traditional agencies do with their big investments in talent, processes, and overhead like real estate. Egos, too, are jettisoned because the best idea comes from anywhere in its network. "We're trying to create a new operating system for the advertising industry," said John Winsor, founder of Victors & Spoils told Ad Age. "We're trying to create a meritocracy." It's a sexy idea for a lot of brands, something that the holding company Havas cottoned to: It bought Victors & Spoils last year for an unknown sum.

There are other spins on this model as well. Co:Collective, started in 2010 by a pair of big agency vets, now consists of a small group of consultants and a roster of over 40 outside partners known as "Co:conspirators." These companies range from Behance (acquired by Adobe in 2012) and Cool Hunting to Naked Communications and Made by Many. For its work on brands' business problems, Co gets a retainer, a fee, or equity, but doesn't skim off the partners' work. As a business, this offers the partners a lot of flexibility, and as a business solution for clients, it offers a wide range of possible strategic and executional paths.

Crowdsourcing—or, really, expert sourcing as Winsor calls it—isn't right for every brand or agency in every situation, but there are attributes that everyone needs to take away. Agencies need to be more open to collaboration than they ever have been and that collaboration will take place with multiple partners:

- Other agencies
- Production partners
- Technology partners
- Influencers
- Freelance experts
- Consumers

That list covers just external collaboration opportunities. More collaboration has to go inside agencies as well. For instance, tech teams are typically looking for final concept from creatives before they write code; they often hate refactoring. The creatives, meanwhile, want to come up with perfect vision before they hand it over. When both sides are immovable on this, it's a recipe for delays. We've found that Agile processes, with their short sprints and incremental delivery, can be a remedy here. We'll talk about that at length in the final part where we describe our convergence road map. For now, the important point is that intra-agency and interagency collaboration is the future.

Brands as Services

Readers of a certain age will remember Special K's "Can't pinch an inch" commercials from the 1970s and 1980s, reminding us that the breakfast cereal can be a weight loss force. Since then, parent Kellogg's has bet big on the Special K brand's healthful associations, extending the brand with meal replacement bars and shakes and variety of snacks and chips. In 2003, the Special K Challenge appeared, motivating consumers to lose 6 pounds in two weeks by eating two Special K product meals per day along with one normal meal. By 2012 the consumer needs had evolved. Whilst many still wanted to kick-start their weight loss with the Special K challenge, many were also looking for longer term solutions—solutions with greater flexibility that meant they could stick with them for longer.

The Special K brand had discovered that women were looking for long-term plans, not just sprints. Said one, "Weight management to me is a never-ending battle." Essentially, they wanted weight management, not just a quick fix. And Special K came to understand that developing the relationship with the customer it wanted hinged on its ability to be there for its consumers over time.

Enter the era of brand as service. For decades, branding was mainly interruptive—commercials that popped up during your favorite TV programming. With limited media and product choice and little opportunity for consumers to voice dismay, brands could get by with a promotional mind-set. Now there has to be a full-time commitment to helping the consumer achieve his or her goals if the brand wants to remain relevant. Otherwise, someone else will. It's not only about getting people to buy something (although that's part of it, of course), it's about helping people to achieve something.

Central to this is the API. The API—or application programming interface—allows software programs to talk to each other, creating new, exciting, and useful experiences for consumers. Over the years, we've been insistent that enterprises need to be part of the open API movement that really took off when Facebook and Twitter opened up their platforms to third-party developers. Google has been slow to issue APIs for its social network Google+, leading to much criticism and speculation that it's held back the growth of the network. This is in contrast to Amazon, which under Jeff Bezos's direction opened up APIs and became a massive marketplace.

More and more companies have gone the way of Amazon, Twitter, and Facebook, opening the door to their systems and data in strategic ways. As of last August, the website ProgrammableWeb had 7,000 APIs in its directory, having added as many in the previous year as in the six years before that. Among them were Zappos, RadioShack, Sears, Tesco, and Etsy. By the time you read this, total APIs will probably be in excess of 8,000.

For our Mercedes Tweet Race program, we made heavy use of APIs and the results were stark. The Tweet Race turned out to be a hit in both social media and mainstream media, amassing some great metrics. The Twitter following grew to more than 77,000 and generated more than 545 million Twitter impressions from 21,000 active participants. There were 72,000 Facebook likes, 2 million video views, and 143 million PR impressions. The business goal to raise brand appeal among the Gen Y audience was achieved by a 5 percent increase in site visitors under the age of 34 in a precampaign/postcampaign survey.

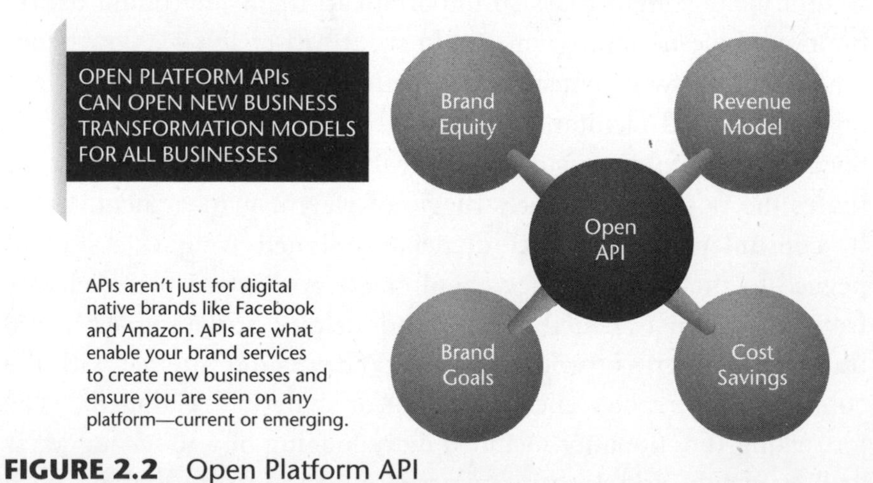

FIGURE 2.2 Open Platform API

Open APIs put you on a fast track to innovation by embracing open APIs and exposing their core business functionality and data to the technology community, where an entire new ecosystem of applications and integrations has emerged. Facebook's authentication API, for example, has become the de facto standard for logging in online.

A great example here is Nike. Nike still does its big, flashy TV ads, but it's becoming increasingly known for its tech services. Its Nike+ FuelBand is about giving people data on their physical activity. The tool is a digital bracelet that employs an accelerometer that measures movement in NikeFuel, what the company describes as "a universal metric of activity." You can then set goals and sync with the FuelBand app to track your history. At last year's South by Southwest, Nike used the FuelBand launch as an opportunity to open up its first API, sponsoring an all-day hackathon so that developers could figure out how to unlock all that data and use it for new applications. Later, one funny hack connected the bracelet to a Twitter account and an Arduino-controlled mechanism that gives a good shake every time there is a new retweet, follow, or mention. Sure it's cheating, but it's funny, too. The takeaway is that when a brand as revered as Nike sees the importance of reaching out to third-party developers, you probably should as well.

Let's get back to our Special K story. To help consumers do the weight management that's so important to them, the brand had to build a whole new program. To do so, it API-enabled its own content assets, allowing consumers to better access the same from various devices and facilitating personalized plans. The result was My Special K, a flexible, customizable, feature-rich program that accentuates the positive, not the struggle of weight management. Using it, consumers could select dietician-designed weight loss plans pegged to their needs. They could create goal-based plans, choose from nutritionist-created recipes and helpful shopping lists, and track their progress through journals. They could interact with the community to receive encouragement or share in social media. The journaling functionality included daily logging of a user's mood, as well as weight and exercise, which connected to the brand's push to have participants focus on the emotional gains associated with weight loss—and not get obsessed with the scale. This was a position that was backed up in the TV campaigns that accompanied the launch.

The personalized daily eating regimens were based on a host of factors, including three lifestyle options: on-the-go, foodie, or vegetarian. Other factors included caloric needs based on gender and age, typical physical activity level, and height and weight. These data, considered alongside the individual's goal date, helps determine a reasonable, healthy weight loss goal for the period specified.

The program also offers registrants/participants access to support from the brand community and social media sharing, customized support newsletters, coupons, and journaling. The results were clear. There were 147 percent year-over-year gains in the program, with 27 percent less media spending. For the first time, 50 percent of users were going beyond the two-week challenge. Good news for Kellogg's, because those who engage in long-term plans spend more on Special K products, which figure heavily in the recipes and menus. Sales increase 114 percent for every two weeks a woman stays on the plan.

If there's a through-line slashing in all of the ideas and work we've discussed in this chapter, it's that next-generation storytelling represents the blurring of the line between technology and creativity. It's no longer about dropping ads into preexisting buckets; it's shaping and reshaping the buckets in the effort to create real value for consumers. A useful mantra here comes from Eric Ries's book, *The Lean Startup:* "Lean thinking defines value as providing benefit to the consumer; anything else is just waste." The reference here is to Agile methodology, a way of thinking about your processes that we'll discuss more in the final chapters. The key thing to remember is customer-centricity.

As you go further down this path, you may ask yourself or your team, "Just what are we building here? Is this an app or ad?"

You don't have to decide on one of these.

You need to build both.

Convergence Catalysts

- Boil your desired social engagement results down to one action sentence:

  "We want [community] to [action] with [object] on [platform] so that [business objective]."

  "We want first-time moms to donate with thank-you points on BabyCenter so that redemption rates of thank-you points are accelerated in specific merchandise categories."
- Open up your APIs—and take advantage of others' APIs. has provided APIs for products, stores, reviews, and more, allowing developers to create platforms that could lead to more business for the retailer. Meanwhile, open is the name of the game with social platforms. Think about how you can leverage that to create new and exciting experiences.
- Reimagine your brand as a problem solver in the life of your client. Ask yourself, what needs does it address, and how can I use technology to facilitate that process?
- Partner early with platforms. Get out of the mind-set that a new technology or platform needs to have a billion users before you start thinking about putting your brand there.
- Rapid prototype. As mentioned above, both Pepperidge Farm and Chrysler, among others, were prototyping with Windows 8 before launch. This had to happen quickly given the launch timeline and they were able to meet the deadline. While designing and building Tweet Race, we were prototyping with APIs and real functionality from the beginning. This helped us design something meaningful for customers, which is critical when building something never done before, like we did with the world's first Twitter-fueled car race.

Data-Driven Experiences

As we write, there is no shortage of evidence pointing to the conclusion that the ability to understand and use big data is increasingly one of the best differentiators for any organization.

Consider the events of fall 2012:

- President Obama rode to reelection on the strength of his campaign's ability to organize and crunch large amounts of voter data.
- Blogger Nate Silver, whose statistical acumen had just predicted the state-by-state outcome of a second presidential election, was getting about as many kudos as the reelected Obama. In a great moment of geek chic, he appeared on the *Colbert Report*, trended on Twitter, and became a meme himself when thousands took to playing "Drunk Nate Silver."
- Major League Baseball's San Francisco Giants demonstrated that the Oakland A's aren't the only ones using *Moneyball*-style analyses of players for better results. The Giants won the World Series for the second time in three years, a mini-dynasty in part attributable to a state-of-the-art system that tracks how well fielders play hit balls and make throws. Incidentally, the team's commitment to tech is long term—they were also first to have Wi-Fi in their stadium and invest in iPads for the locker

room. And one of their key executives is a guy named Yeshayah Goldfarb, who possesses a very un-baseball-like title: director of minor league operations/quantitative analysis.

- The *Harvard Business Review,* in an issue that featured big data on the cover, called the data scientist "the sexiest job of the twenty-first century."

With more than 2.5 exabytes of data created each day, a number that's doubling every 40 months, there is quite literally a glut of information about the world that can inform every decision that a business makes. It's a good time to be in data, a fact that the marketing world is only slowly waking up to. Enterprises are getting better at using this information, and data-driven experiences are on the increase, but not growing as fast as we'd like to see. A lot of work remains to be done.

Hesitancy remains to really engage with data-driven programs despite early indications that there is a correlation between being data-driven and positive business performance, as shown by a

Data-driven marketing provides significant opportunities to listen and connect with consumers and businesses in ways not possible before.

FIGURE 3.1 Looking Ahead

recent MIT survey of executives at 330 public companies. "The more companies characterized themselves as data-driven, the better they performed on objective measures of financial and operational results," read the study. "In particular, companies in the top-third of their industry in the use of data-driven decision-making were, on average, 5 percent more productive and 6 percent more profitable than their competitors." That advantage takes into account contributions, labor, capital, services, and IT investment. And there may be even more opportunity than that. A McKinsey study has asserted that big data could also enable retailers to increase their operating margins by as much as 60 percent. At one of our retail clients, the company saw a 25 percent lift after simply adding data-driven recommended products.

Some companies have already realized this:

- Since Tesco launched its loyalty program back in 1995, the U.K.-based retailer has been a big believer in big data, using it not only to keep customers friendly but to help manage its supply chain. Data crunching has led to improved promotions, resulting in 30 percent fewer gaps on store shelves. Predicting weather and understanding how it affects consumer behavior has meant £6 million less of food wastage in the summer, £50 million less worth of stock in warehouses, and optimization of store operations that resulted in £30 million less waste.
- Sears Holdings takes its huge quantities of customer, product, and promotion data from brands to generate personalized promotions. All the processing once took eight weeks because the data had to be ported in from various warehouses, meaning the insights often got stale. To speed things up, it built a Hadoop cluster to store incoming data from all brands and analyzed the cluster directly in a manner that was much faster and more precise. Time required dropped from eight weeks to one.
- The upscale retailer Williams-Sonoma, which has bet big on marketing attribution, uses big data techniques to create

> customized campaigns for the individual based on models to determine what kind of marketing stream (direct mail versus e-mail versus banner ads) makes sense for what kind of customer. "Big data changed our entire dynamics," said Williams-Sonoma CIO John Strain in 2012. "We can calculate hundreds of predictive attributes and leverage our spending to each channel."

Despite these stories, we see a gulf between talk and action when it comes to data—and we're not the only ones. A study last year by the Columbia Business School and New York American Marketing Association found that almost all of the senior marketing executives surveyed believe that successful brands use data to drive decision making. The good news here is that the marketing industry's long-standing insistence that it's more about art and gut feeling and abstract notions of creativity than numbers seems to have weakened. Finally, the industry is talking the right talk.

And now for the bad news. Thirty-nine percent admitted that their organization's data is collected too infrequently or slowly, and just over half said that poor sharing of data has been a bar to using data effectively. Drilling deeper into the study, we read that data collection remains a problem. Almost 30 percent said their marketing departments take in little or no data. Only 19 percent of companies collected mobile device data, and social media data—easy and cheap as such data is to collect—were collected by only 35 percent. Compare that to customer survey data on demographics (74 percent) and attitudes (54 percent), and you've got a rather bleak portrait of the contemporary marketing industry's relationship with data. Lots of big talk with little real activity.

"We found that so far, big data in marketing is still a work in progress," wrote the survey authors. "In many organizations, the effective use of data for marketing decisions lags behind the desire to do so."

Data that is reflective of vast amounts of actual, lived customer behavior are increasingly informing customer experiences for a growing list of enlightened brands, but that list isn't as long as it should be. Companies such as Netflix and Amazon, founded at the dawn of the digital age, had data encoded into their DNA. Many older companies haven't acted as quickly as they might have. They're bogged down by legacy systems they struggle to bring together, they haven't found the ROI, or it's simply not part of their culture. There is still widespread—and misguided—thinking that organizations are either right-brained or left-brained, with little room for compromise between the lobes. Our own research, conducted with Adobe, shows just how slow companies have been to use data even from and on their own websites. We'll get to that later.

In the meantime, we'll argue that these objections are wrongheaded, that resistance to data is not only futile but foolish. The fact of the matter is that if your organization doesn't figure out how to collect, process, and effectively use the rapidly growing amounts of data currently available, then someone else will. An age of data-driven disruption is at hand.

> An age of data-driven disruption is at hand.

If you want to see how this is happening, just look at the media business, where cultural and institutional resistance have turned things upside down. Venerable newspaper and magazine publishers, in just the course of a few years, have seen their audiences, once thought of as massive, get dwarfed by startups born with a priori understanding of how to use data that could be possessed by only digitally native companies. As of September 2011, the then-four-year-old *Business Insider* was getting almost double the traffic of the *Wall Street Journal* with just a fraction of the investment in editorial resources. Why? Besides eschewing a paywall, *Business Insider* was obsessed with traffic data, allowing it to determine not only what stories to publish but how they are headlined and promoted in social media. Similar strategies have been employed at the *Huffington Post,* where the A/B testing of the headlines is a routine practice: The one that gets the most clicks get used. BuzzFeed, the media sensation of last year founded by *Post* cofounder Jonah Peretti, is known for its masterful use of social media optimization to send its highly shared lists about cute animals around the Web. Whereas Amazon has a good idea of what you might like to buy, BuzzFeed understands what you're likely to click on and share. But BuzzFeed is also a master of data. Its measurement dashboard is traded to rivals such as *Time, Fox News,* and the *Huffington Post* in exchange for their audience data. And last September it purchased Kingfish Labs. Why? To study what makes something go viral on Facebook. For a twenty-first-century media company, it's not enough to have good editors—you have to have the data, too, and you have to use it.

Other industries will follow suit and we will see winners and losers determined in no small part by whether and how they organize for data. It's no longer enough to rely on predigital ways of planning and measuring. Putting Web analytics at the center of an operation is only the first layer, and a straightforward one at that. Zillow has disrupted the real estate market by building the largest database of home prices around, offering transparency where there was none before. Airbnb and Kayak have done much the same for the travel industry. Facebook is matching branded content to receptive consumers through constant optimization of its News Feed.

Data, as we see it, is at once disruptive and empowering. Enterprises that sell products and services have more complex data challenges than do media companies that are generally in the business of seeking out audiences. In this chapter, we'll explore how those challenges can be met through Staples, one of our more advanced clients when it comes to data.

At the same time, we'll be sure to remind you that the quantity hasn't totally killed the quality. Smart and comprehensive data strategies don't replace strong right-brain thinking. They tell you what creative output works when and with whom. The trick is getting the creative directors to go along with data-driven insights. As BuzzFeed's Peretti has said in *Fast Company*, "There's art and science to it. The math helps you have better understanding and helps you have more creative ideas, but you can't replace the creative ideas."

Shantanu Narayen, CEO of Adobe, echoed this. When we complained that too many businesses were slow to make investments in data, Narayen wisely suggested that we may have just seen "a watershed moment in how you use data to spend money online."

He wasn't talking about any business.

He was talking about a political campaign.

How Obama Used Data to Keep the White House

In 2008, when Barack Obama came out of nowhere to become the first African American president of the United States, two main reasons were given for his triumph: a macro message of hope and change that got large swathes of voters excited and a technological prowess theretofore not seen in politics. Obama's success in digital channels, where he cultivated massive communities, gave him a leg up on a McCain campaign that seemed like it was still struggling to set up an AOL e-mail account. He made short work of the Republican candidate.

But the reality, unbeknownst to anyone until years after, is that the Obama campaign actually had one gaping flaw that might have been disastrous for its reelection efforts had it not been fixed: It had too many databases. And to make matters worse, each of those databases was lorded over by campaign unit managers who were very protective of them. Here how the problem netted out, according to *Slate:* "They had records on 170 million potential voters, 13 million online supporters, 3 million campaign donors and at least as many volunteers—but no way of knowing who among them were the same people."

In 2012, the Obama campaign fixed those problems and erased a recent Republican advantage when it came to figuring out how to turn data crunching into electoral success. The key to George W. Bush's electoral success was the segmentation strategies carried out by GOP guru Karl Rove, a direct marketer by trade. Obama flipped the script, turning numbers crunching into a strength for the Democratic Party as it navigated a very divided electoral map. We propose this as an object lesson in the power of data, as an example of what can happen when leadership, culture, and technology line up behind data-driven decision making.

Obama's reelection campaign effort began with a clean slate datawise, and created, according to *Time* magazine, "a single massive system that could merge the information collected from pollsters, fund-raisers, field workers, and consumer databases as well as social-media and mobile contacts with the main Democratic voter files in the swing states." Moreover, that database was available to anyone in the campaign.

The impact was incredible. The database told the campaign when a donor had the hit the maximum dollar allowed by federal law so that he or she could then be targeted as a volunteer. It allowed for targeted messaging, say, leaving antiabortion voters off e-mail blasts with prochoice content. It identified celebrities such as George Clooney and Sarah Jessica Parker as the right ones to take part in fund-raising dinners. It informed media buys, telling the campaign's media buyers that instead of local news placement, ads might be more effective at reaching target voters if they were in TV programming such as *Sons of Anarchy* and *The Walking Dead*. "On TV we were able to buy 14 percent more efficiently," one unnamed official told *Time*, "to make sure we were talking to our persuadable voters."

Data analysis even told the campaign's writers that sometimes spammy-sounding e-mail subject lines ("Real quick," "Hey," "Let's grab some coffee") worked and, presumably, that they should feel free to make them ever weirder.

Voters in battleground states were all assigned persuadability scores that told the campaign whether they were worth bothering with and how they should be approached. It allowed the campaign to create better-informed microsegments out of a large undifferentiated group like "undecided voters."

Wrote *ProPublica:* "To pinpoint voters who might actually change their minds, the Obama campaign conducted randomized experiments. . . . Voters received phone calls in which they were asked to rate their support for the president, and then engaged in a conversation about different policy issues. At the end of the conversation, they were asked to rate their support for the president again. Using the results of these experiments, combined with detailed demographic information about individual voters, the campaign was able to pinpoint both what kinds of voters had been persuaded to support the president, and which issues had persuaded them."

A key figure in all this was Rayid Ghani, the campaign's chief scientist and a former Accenture researcher. He oversaw a project called Dreamcatcher that was a big bet on textual analytics, a systematic effort to determine patterns in all of the personal information and stories collected throughout the campaign, from a canvasser's clipboard to a call center conversation to the Share Your Story function on the campaign website.

Another key figure was campaign manager Jim Messina, whose commonsense approach to data set the tone in BuzzFeed. "You have to test every single thing, to challenge every assumption, and to make sure that everything we do is provable," Messina said. "That's why I love numbers. Because you know good or bad whether what you're doing is working." The campaign put money where its mouth was, investing $100 million in IT, widely believed to be unparalleled in politics.

And the campaign shifted priorities in terms of what it was listening to, improving the signal-to-noise ratio. An early step was ignoring national polls in favor of state and local ones, and in particular ditching Gallup, the esteemed national polling service, which predicted that minorities and young voters would turn out to vote in fewer numbers. Gallup was wrong. The campaign's own computer simulation would run the election 66,000 times a night and then the next day rejigger investments based on those simulations. These simulations predicted both Ohio and Florida, two of the largest swing states, within one-half of 1 percent, and they were only off on one state, Colorado, where Obama did better than the simulation predicted.

The Romney campaign didn't ignore data, but it did struggle with data analysis at crucial moments. On election day, an app designed to give the campaign real-time analytics about voter turnout in crucial precincts wasn't just clunky; it crashed. Orca, the campaign's name for the project, gave volunteers in the swing states a mobile Web app allowing them to report back to Romney headquarters about voter turnout in important precincts. Based on that information, the campaign would be able to bombard voters with phone calls, urging them to cast their ballots.

That was how it was supposed to work; in practice, it turned out to be a very different experience. The volunteers were poorly trained, and there were problems with the hosting setup. Rather than put it in the cloud, the program was hosted on virtual machines, believed to be in or around Boston Garden, where the war room was located. As a result, the Orca Web page was routinely inaccessible. There was a panoply of other IT problems as well, from invalid passwords to poor application testing that didn't put the user experience through the proper paces. By 4 PM on the big day, Orca, hastily designed and poorly deployed, had crashed.

Rather than empower the Romney ground game, it decimated its volunteers' morale. Wrote one volunteer on his blog, "So, the end result was that 30,000+ of the most active and fired-up volunteers were wandering around confused and frustrated when they could have been doing anything else to help. Like driving people to the polls, phone-banking, walking door-to-door, etc. We lost by fairly small margins in Florida, Virginia, Ohio and Colorado. If this had worked could it have closed the gap? I sure hope not for my sanity's sake."

Wrote John Dickerson in a postmortem for *Slate:* "In the final 10 days of the race, a split started to emerge in the two campaigns. The Obama team would shower you with a flurry of data—specific, measurable, and they'd show you the way they did the math. Any request for written proof was immediately filled. They knew their brief so well you could imagine Romney hiring them to work at Bain. The Romney team, by contrast, was much more gauzy, reluctant to share numbers, and relying on talking points rather than data."

There you have it: two campaigns, two approaches to data, one winner. At a panel shortly after the election, Romney aide Brian Jones argued that his candidate "won on the vision for the future, on being a strong leader, on the deficit." Then he added, "Ultimately, though, it just didn't matter. These guys just ran an incredibly proficient and strong and well-organized campaign. We had a little bit of the edge on the macro-messaging, but it just didn't matter."

The lessons for a business enterprise are clear. Many companies, after all, are faced with challenges similar to those the Obama campaign faced after the 2008 victory, especially data living in many different silos and on several systems that don't talk well to each other.

That efficiency that Jones mentioned goes back to the decision made by the campaign to integrate its data and change the organization's culture and priorities. And this doesn't have to be a glacial undertaking. The Obama campaign did it in a matter of several months and, in the process, overtook the Republican Party's edge in data. To do so, it needed investment, people, and mind-set.

The Road to Marketing Utopia Is Lined with Columns and Rows

How can we take the contemporary political approach to data—which we can sum up as a big sloppy embrace—and apply it to enterprises? This is an enormously complex problem that very few companies have figured out. Injecting data-driven mind-sets, processes, and cultures into enterprises isn't easy, and it's that much more difficult for companies that predate the big data boom. But that doesn't mean it can't be done.

To understand how one company is doing it, let's look at Staples, the 25-year-old office supply company based in Framingham, Massachusetts. Our client there is Kevin Biondi, who, as director of global digital marketing, oversees digital strategy and execution across Staples brands. He's been at the company since 2009, arriving from the financial services sector, where he did stints at JP Morgan Chase and Citigroup.

Biondi is laser focused on helping consumers find what they need as quickly as possible. Scratch that—he is, more accurately, trying to help consumers and business owners find things they need that they don't yet know that they need. And, no, he is not a psychic. He is simply putting data to work for his organization.

The broad shift is toward personalization, using data to get as close as possible to what your consumer wants.

Imagine the small business customer who shows up at the website looking for a few printer ink cartridges. Some real-time data analysis may determine that a better solution for the customer might be a managed print service. Or what about the shopper who thinks she wants a 1-terabyte hard drive? Maybe a cloud storage service would work better.

This sort of thing isn't about upselling the customer—it's something bigger. "It's not just what they need, but how do we help them scale their overarching business," Biondi said.

Getting there isn't easy and Biondi is quick to talk about the challenges. He says that there are two main challenges for data.

The first is speed. The shelf life of a data point is short; its value deteriorates quickly. As a result, being fast to market is critical, and the data-driven insight is critical.

The second challenge is this, as Biondi puts it: "There is so much data. How do you approach and interpret the data into actual, meaningful insights?"

There are any number of ways to articulate the data deluge. There's Walmart's 1 million customer transactions every hour, filling databases already teeming with more than 2.5 petabytes of data. There's the fast growth of unstructured data, including the 48 hours of video uploaded to YouTube every minute of the day, the 571 new websites created, or the 100 terabytes of data uploaded to Facebook on a daily basis.

Daunting as it might be, the beauty of all this data is that it allows you to get to that true one-to-one relationship, if you know what to do with it. Biondi said, "The thing we really need to size up is how do you build that one mega data solution that pipes in data from all the sources that makes it sensible and clean?"

The salve here is automation, but the reality, says Biondi, is that the data deluge is so constant and expansive that automation always lags behind. There's an analogy in the search engine optimization's function, as SEO techniques are in a constant game of catch-up with the Google algorithm. Just when they figure it out, the algorithm changes. Not only does the algorithm change, but remember that with Google's Panda release in early 2012, all Google users have unique search results based on their usage.

Some organizations have taken this even further. In recent years, we've seen a smattering of chief data officers pop up on the scene. The short list of companies that have used the role includes Capital One, Yahoo!, and Citigroup. Major cities, including New York, San Francisco, and Chicago, have also adopted it. These aren't necessarily direct reports to the CEO; often the report is to the CIO or CTO. The job consists of setting priorities around data and making sure that the challenges described earlier are being met head-on. Whether it makes sense depends on the specific case, but the point is clear: Using data brings significant organizational challenges.

But using it successfully helps you to be more responsive to the wants and needs of your customers. After all, an organization that is paying attention to data is an organization that is listening to its customers. "It's not about data-driven marketing," Biondi told us. "It's about hearing from the customer in a mass way."

As recently as 10 or 12 years ago, if you wanted to hear what your customers were thinking or saying, you had to field an old-school market research tool such as a focus group. The problem was that there were many, all stemming from the fact that focus groups are artificial environments that yield unscientific results. Here's behavioral economist Dan Ariely on focus groups: "Think about what a strange idea it is that we take 10 people who know basically nothing about your project and you put them in the room and you let them talk for a while and then you take the . . . whatever they came up with, as a consequence of these two hours of random thinking and you base your strategy on it, to a large degree." Ariely allows that focus groups are useful in corporate environments to persuade people that such groups are not terribly useful as a way to obtain information. Essentially, they become political tools used to justify activity, not methods to understand consumer behavior in a way that informs or determines what actions the organization should take. The feedback they provide just isn't that reliable.

"What customers say in the focus group is very different from what they actually do," said Biondi. "It speaks to knowing what they will do versus having someone talk about their thoughts. Focus groups are good for perceptions, but it's the data that gives you more reality."

That's because the data come from actual experience, whether Web-browsing history or purchasing behavior. It's not about what consumers say but rather about what they do.

Looking at the world this way inevitably leads you rethink how you segment your customer base. Staples, Biondi said, has grown less reliant on traditional demographic segments and is paying more attention to customer behavioral segments that can be derived from digital data. And that brings its own complications. Behavioral ad data have a much wider net than your CRM database, enabling greater reach and testability.

For one thing, the number of segments you deal with grows and you have to strike a balance between the potential of endless segmentation possibilities and the need to get stuff done.

"For it to be truly personalized, you're not talking about just a thousand segments but tens of thousands of segments of customers," he said. "There are probably millions of segments. You really have to evaluate the effort versus the impact. You have a lot of data and you can get a lot of insights, but you have to ask whether it's scalable enough to spend the time on analyzing that data. You don't want to slow the organization down."

We're the first to admit there are no easy answers here. But at least Biondi and Staples are in the game when so many are sitting on the sidelines.

How Targeting Is Failing Consumers

The Amazon.com user experience is both familiar and foreign. It's familiar because we've all used it, and it's foreign because so few other companies have learned from it.

To see what we mean, go to the site. Assuming you've got an account and you're logged in, you'll be met with a wealth of product offerings. As we write, Amazon is heavily pushing its new Kindle Fire tablet and its Paperwhite e-reader to all shoppers and come-ons for those products are posted prominently atop the page. It's as "dumb" as the experience gets, for as you scroll down, you're inevitably met with products that are there only because they relate to actions you've taken—items you've recently looked at, items inspired by your browsing history, items that others who share your purchasing behavior have purchased. The effect is to create an often-irresistible palette of products and, with it, a feeling of uncanniness: How did they know I wanted something I didn't even know existed?

This veritable cornucopia of smart recommendations is what has made Amazon the $102 billion company it is today. As much as 30 percent of the company's sales have been attributed to its recommendation engine, which, while far from perfect, is a central part of the Amazon experience.

That's the Amazon experience, best summed up as the feeling that the company knows you or at least a little about you, and that it values the data it has. Now let's look at the more typical corporate website experience.

Imagine a typical Web user. Let's call him Gary. Gary fires up his browser and visits his favorite clothing retailer in search of that perfect shirt/pant/tie combo to wear to his first day at the new job. He's what you might call a brand loyalist—he's even got a branded platinum credit card.

As he scrolls through the site, Gary winces at some of the trendy clothes on display. The retailer is trying to sell him stuff he'll never buy because he's always been conservative when it comes to his wardrobe. He spends 20 minutes searching the areas of the site that carry the clothes he likes, finds the perfect outfit, and three clicks later, is awaiting free delivery. Experience complete.

If we dissect this visit, it's clear that Gary's experience—that of a loyal customer—is undifferentiated. Gary isn't being treated like a known customer. There's no targeted experience at his fingertips. Why? Because even though he visits the site frequently and tells the retailer what's important to him through what he clicks on and purchases, to say nothing of what his browsing history tells him, the retailer isn't paying attention or learning from his previous visits. What does this mean? For Gary, it might not mean much—until another company vies for his attention with an experience that shows it has been paying attention. At risk is a lost opportunity for engagement and perhaps lost revenue.

This inattention to the question of customer data may seem exaggerated, but we found in a recent study that it's anything but. By and large, companies are falling down on a foundational data–based marketing activity: targeting owned digital assets, such as the company website, where you have direct influence over both content and user experience. Site-side targeting goes far beyond user authentication on your site or loyalty program subscription, although those are both important attributes of sound data collection. When we reference site-side targeting across owned digital channels, we mean listening to our customers and applying that feedback to future interactions. This is about knowing where a customer accesses the site, what they looked at during their last two visits, and predicting how to translate that information into a better experience by utilizing the most relevant content on their next visit.

By combining CRM loyalty data and ad-serving behavioral data with third-party audience data, we've seen big data–fueled targeting implementations yield triple-digit ROI increases for multiple clients. To deliver these meaningful experiences in real time, businesses need to fully assess their business readiness—including customer strategy, technology, analytics, and data-informed dynamic creative delivery. We built a targeting readiness framework to assess a company's ability to capture data (platform), analyze that data for insights (analytics), and empower the business to develop those insights into tailored content (activation) that is realized in a unique customer experience.

Razorfish and Adobe applied this framework to a survey that was composed of 120 marketing, technology, and business executives who are key decision makers of their owned properties at companies with revenues exceeding $500 million. The goal: to determine whether a business has what it takes to succeed at each progressive stage of targeting across owned digital properties.

The study revealed that:

- Business leaders are using traditional predigital methods of segmentation, relying largely on historic sales data and missing the opportunity to apply behavioral data learning, which is the core of meaningful digital experiences.
- Using traditional data has led to a status quo where acquiring customers is the primary goal. The creation of tailored experiences doesn't get enough attention, resulting in lower conversion and wasted advertising dollars.
- The digital landscape is changing so fast that companies are struggling to determine which digital channels are in their control—often resulting in missed opportunities to create a holistic customer experience perspective.

- Internal barriers, which include technology and organizational support costs, stop executives from further developing their customer targeting capabilities.

We expected to see more businesses demonstrating maturity with their site-side segmentation capabilities, especially since 49 percent of survey respondents consider themselves strong at targeting experiences to segmented groups of online audiences. Surprisingly, only 12 percent have implemented the ability to target a recognized segment and measure the results. Just 56 percent of companies said that they were in the early stages of developing analytics capabilities, and less than 50 percent were able to recognize a returning/loyal customer versus a prospect. Another 64 percent of businesses are only in the early stages of developing a set of metrics to gauge targeting success, which means that even those who believe they have strong targeting capabilities may not be able to quantify that value.

When we looked at sophistication of data integration and analysis, we found that only 15 percent of respondents are actually in an optimized position, and 62 percent rely solely on historic sales and customer profile data to drive segmentation and targeting activities. These brands are missing the human element of consumption—behavioral data—that is largely found through analysis of site-side digital measurement. At a basic level, Web metrics and more complex first- and third-party cookie level data is combined to tell the story of the entire customer experience.

We looked closely at organizations that rated themselves a four or five in their segmentation maturity in order to understand their owned-asset targeting. Of that subset of respondents, there was a distinct divide—what we call the segmentation divide—with only 36 percent able to deliver a targeted experience to a recognized customer.

When we consider the technology that these organizations are investigating or deploying, we see that many are investigating capabilities for site-side targeting, but few have actually implemented targeting capabilities beyond just insights and analytics.

Clearly, there's a disconnect between what data are being used to develop what executives consider to be strong targeted experiences and how those data points are analyzed, segmented, and delivered for targeting.

This lack of targeted experiences could be due to the fact that 58 percent of respondents have defined and implemented a strategy for creative/content development for dynamic reuse, and only 32 percent said that their digital ecosystem could support dynamically delivered content across channels.

From this perspective, segmentation is being leveraged mainly for analysis in silos, rather than for creating tailored experiences. This is a pity because it's not the technology but how you use it that will define success.

Executives Fail to Prioritize Targeting

When we asked respondents to tell us how they prioritize their efforts to meet customer expectations, we found that in general, there was a strong focus on improving interactions between channels. Depending on the role within the organization, however, executive priorities differed: CEOs focused on implementing real-time communication, CTOs tried to stay ahead of privacy concerns, and CIOs and CMOs focused heavily on immediate responsiveness across channels. Surprisingly, our study revealed that personalization is lowest on the priority scale—personalization being a direct result of better-targeted content and experiences in owned channels.

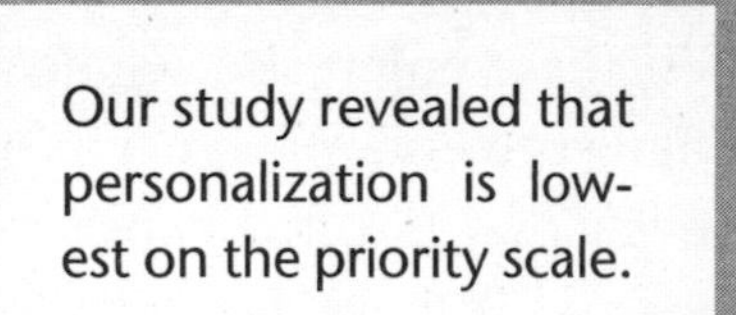

Making personalization such a low priority is almost a rebuke to the approach that's made Amazon so great.

This lack of prioritization is evident in the lack of maturity or ability to target, since only 12 percent claim to have the ability to target a specific customer segment and measure results for optimization.

The survey tells us that targeting uses traditional methods of segmentation analysis to fuel digital experiences. We see an executive disconnect between segmentation development and digital execution because 55 percent can't use their data to tell which customers to grow, win back, retain, or acquire—and 52 percent believe that they are in the early stages of recognizing a customer against their segmentation strategy and delivering a targeted experience.

Most of our clients ask us to work with an existing enterprise segmentation model on one end of the spectrum. These typically are persona profiles, which range between 5 and 10 segments. Meanwhile, there are a myriad of data points on the opposite end of the spectrum, with some aligned to the segments and others—including behavioral data—captured but not analyzed. What this translates to is an avid acquisition play, where display and traditional media are targeted toward the defined enterprise segments that have traditionally yielded the highest return. Often, we find that this approach focuses on total revenue per segment, rather than deeper inquiries into metrics like the lifetime value, which tells a more holistic story of a customer, including how much to spend to acquire them and what their ongoing relationship with the business means.

Once we apply rigorous analysis on nonpersonally identifiable information, along with ongoing testing and optimization activities, these enterprise segments tend to become more granular, and microsegments emerge. Once there is more segment granularity, the power of a targeted experience becomes meaningful and the business can respond to its customers in a more personal way. A brand with this type of customer insight is no longer focused solely on customer acquisition. These businesses have the opportunity to engage customers and move them further along the purchase funnel into the consideration and trial set—areas of the funnel that our study found to be most lacking in data support.

We recommend that executives evaluate their current segmentation strategy and assess whether they are using traditional means of segmentation to influence digital experiences. Segments are traditionally minded groupings based on demographics; typically, something folks are comfortable keeping in their head. Microsegments are based on machine learning and clustering algorithms and can be much larger in number than traditional segments. One-to-one data-driven messaging and services are based on your specific transactions and attributes.

Does this segmentation take into account behavioral data? Are your digital experiences speaking to the subset of microsegments and their individual needs? If not, we believe that there is room to grow your business capabilities and potentially realize the triple-digit ROI growth we've seen with other clients.

Don't ignore the downstream purchase funnel.

Organizations are more focused on acquisition and service and less on trial, reengagement, and advocacy stages. This suggests that marketers need to redefine the role of each owned channel to meet business goals for (1) all stages of the purchase funnel and (2) its business segments.

By targeting in the advocate stage, there's an opportunity to capitalize by engaging loyalists and giving them something to talk about. Each customer uses each channel differently, and by addressing how attribution and other customer analytics are leveraged to establish where to invest for each target, marketers will be better positioned to hone their content so that it's personalized at every stage of the purchase funnel.

Thanks to technology with predictive capabilities, we've discovered that this focus actually makes it more efficient for marketers to focus on their right/best customers without undue burden. This is achieved by:

- Understanding what customers respond to and implementing technology to continuously test and understand customer preferences.
- Building the content development team so that they are less focused on trying to speak to a broad segment and more focused on tailoring messaging, both visual and text, to the microsegment, which can be tested in small sample sizes for efficiency.

- Creating content assets in parts that can be assembled dynamically through smart content management systems such as Adobe Experience Manager and Adobe Target. This way the same creative components can be reused but served in a way that is more meaningful to a targeted group of consumers.

The opportunities we've articulated thus far can be realized only if there're business support and resources to make them happen. In our study, we found that the largest barriers to realizing greater site-side segmentation are costs associated with technology and people. Interestingly, most respondents didn't consider low expected ROI as a barrier, and only 18 percent considered lack of clear value proposition a hindrance. So the case for site-side segmentation and targeting is understood but is increasingly becoming a competing priority for limited business resources.

We are sensitive to these considerations but also realize that investments in today's technology actually work smarter to deliver value in months, rather than years. When you consider the expense of implementing technology such as Adobe Target, Analytics, and Adobe Experience Manager, compared with the major enterprise CRM implementations of the past, the cost pales in comparison and the ROI timeline is much shorter.

From an organizational standpoint, we also recognize that businesses are built over time and that each area of the business tends to build infrastructure that supports their specific functions. The result is an organization that is siloed by data as much as anything else. Only 24 percent of companies have implemented a process for creative development so that content can be served dynamically and reused across segments. If you're working with a forward-thinking agency, they should easily be able to accomplish this.

Be sure to reassess your current technology.

Before you make the new technology investment plunge, we encourage you to take a close look at your current technology capabilities. We've seen a number of clients who have already invested in great technology options but ultimately abandon those based on functionality, sour vendor relationships, or poor performance against expectations. Many of the smart technology failures we've seen come from missing the key advisory function that bridges business strategy and technology implementation. If you already have technology that you believe can help make better use of your segmentation and content delivery, we encourage you to bring in an outside advisor to assess areas of opportunity. It may mean something as small as team training or optimizing the way features and functions of a technology are currently being used.

As data-driven experiences and businesses continue to prove out their ROI, the new role of a data scientist becomes more and more critical. This role that brings together math and computing science is a hybrid thinker that is just now starting to create a curriculum on how to grow more of these skills.

The Road to Better Targeting

To help you figure out how to create better experiences, we've created a five-step process:

1. **Develop your blueprint for business readiness.** We believe every business will be well served by a customer-targeting blueprint that focuses on how to improve site-side customer experiences. Based on this survey, Razorfish and Adobe developed a framework to assess your targeting readiness and to compare it against a general and industry-specific benchmark.

   The four dimensions of the model presented (platform, analytics, activation, and experience) can help us quickly define areas where you can focus your business to improve your site-side segmentation capabilities. This becomes your site-side targeting blueprint. You can also review your company's performance against that of others in your industry to determine

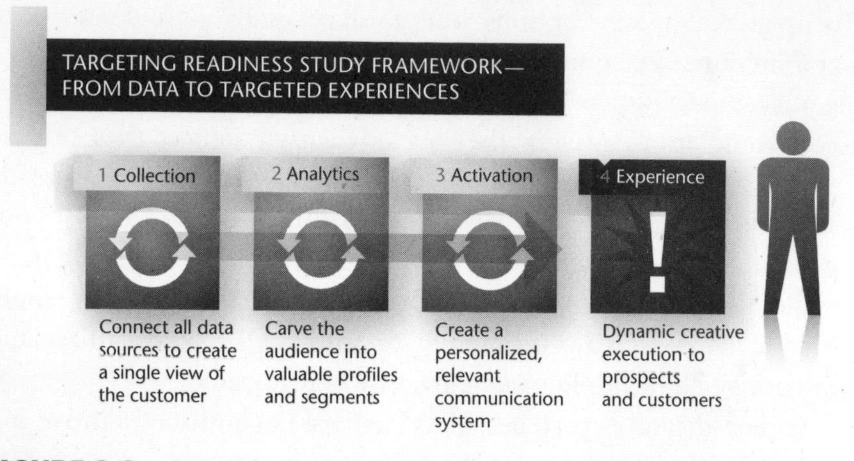

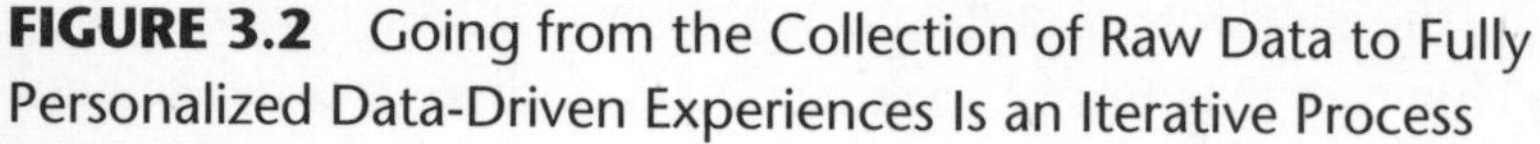
FIGURE 3.2 Going from the Collection of Raw Data to Fully Personalized Data-Driven Experiences Is an Iterative Process

areas where you may achieve competitive advantage. Your unique road map will help siloed teams work toward efficient programs and guarantee that you are bringing customers into an experience that is optimized to meet their needs.

2. **Determine your level of targeting sophistication.** While you assess your business and develop your blueprint, we expect that you will also begin a process of constantly reevaluating your performance across the platform, analytics, activation, and experience dimensions. During this process, we typically see companies progress through the following levels of targeting sophistication:

   Level 1—Cross-channel insights. A unified, cross-channel view of your customer data means that you can then conduct analysis and emerge with a single view of the customer that will fuel future experience and content development.

   Level 2—Informed media. Data from owned properties, combined with enterprise transactional data, is integrated and used to control media bidding and remessaging for off-network personalization. That opens the pathways for more efficient and qualified audience buys for the right kind of prospective customers.

Level 3—Dynamic targeting in a single channel. Data from cross-channel analysis are focused on building experiences, measuring performance within single channels, and being aware that your blueprint will help keep you aligned to the ultimate goal of cross-channel targeting.

Level 4—Dynamic, multichannel targeting. Strong technology platform, advanced analytics, content creation strategy, and organizational support translate into a seamless customer experience, regardless of whether the customer is online or off or which device the customer uses to engage. Follow Google's lead of using all your touchpoints, whether e-mail or search or maps, to create a better experience everywhere. Google Now, for instance, is a virtual personal assistant that will predict what information you might need, say, directions to your lunch meeting or a check-in on the traffic.

Level 5—Multichannel retail and service. Digital is optimized for targeting across all channels and now the focus is making in-person interactions as guided as digital, enabling the sales process, for instance, to start in-store and finish at home.

3. **Drive collaboration among creative and technology teams.** Ask yourself this: When your organization last developed its website, an app, or a social media program—or bought paid media, created retail experiences, or started a customer service channel—how much effort was put into targeting concepts? If the answer is "not much," then you need empowering technology to dynamically assemble content and visual elements. For full desktop, mobile, or application experiences, this can be much more wide-ranging, including using data to improve navigation and search at the intersection of paid and owned channels.

Any use of data targeting without a needs/expectations-based user experience will fall flat. That's where Adobe's vision of combining data-fueled insights with targeted content bridges the data/experience gap. Using Adobe products, we are able to directly tie creative visual and copy content with the targeting data we've captured through various customer touchpoints. In fact, at Razorfish, creative teams can work in the Adobe Creative Suite and Creative Cloud (such as Adobe Photoshop, Adobe InDesign, etc.) and go directly into Adobe Experience Manager, where the new creative can be immediately served to targeted audiences. Marketing capabilities—from strategic through execution—are now essentially stitched together between the infinite ways we can target experiences using data, and the creative producers making the experience delightful.

4. **Think about big technology vendors for complete solutions, but consider solution design expertise to accelerate benefits.** As big technology vendors increasingly make fully integrated solutions possible, organizations that have purchased a best-of-breed solution stack can gain a competitive edge and incremental benefits from partnering with expert solution designers. The difference in realizing those triple-digit percentage ROI benefits we've mentioned is in the way that you piece it all together. Service-oriented technology partners add a unique mix of people and process to your existing teams, propelling technology transformation and innovation without requiring a major overhaul of your day-to-day operations.

By establishing cross-team leadership that includes your in-house teams, technology vendors, and solution design partners, you can leverage existing tried-and-true capabilities, complemented by new technology and software-as-a-service (SaaS) data-integration offerings. The result will be faster returns from your technology investments.

This infusion of new thinking for problem solving can make all the difference when planning the rollout of a platform road map—taking into account your business objectives and readiness to support the delivery of new experiences. So if you're looking to gain greater organizational investment, support greater testing capability in the short term.

5. **Don't forget business strategy.** To establish a vision and maintain focus on targeting for big results, align targeting capabilities behind a single business strategy, a measurement plan, and ongoing learning at the customer level. Integrating cross-channel insights and value management around the customer experience will clarify what activities and investments are required to satisfy your objectives.

   As we have worked with massive numbers of algorithmically discovered consumer segments, it remains critical to keep sight of the business rational behind using data. As some of our clients have reminded us, we don't want to mindlessly blast thousands of segments, but rather use statistics to determine what works for those segments. Historically, marketing efforts were completed when a TV commercial launched, but in the digital world, the starting point is when you launch. The key is to stay focused on your business goals and use the data and technology to confirm your tactics against those goals. The old truism remains: you are more likely to achieve your goals if you simply write them down.

When it comes to data, the time for excuses is over. There are too many examples from the private and public sectors demonstrating the benefits of a data-driven organization. Of course, not every enterprise can become as sophisticated as the Obama campaign was overnight, but at the same time, there's no excuse for not jumping into the pond and creating tailored experiences in owned channels, like your company's website. At this point in history, with sophisticated startups waiting to use data to eat your lunch, can you really afford not to?

You do the math.

Convergence Catalysts

- Create a business strategy for data. What are you trying to achieve and for whom? Play your own private game of *Moneyball*. Ask yourself whether you're measuring the right stuff and how you can be better.
- Begin with your corporate website. Take a good hard look at it and, using the framework we've provided, decide whether you're providing the best experience possible to your consumers. The goal should be an experience shaped to individual consumers, not a static, one-size-fits-all experience.
- If you work for one of the many enterprises that suffer from data fragmentation, consider a task force or a team to better integrate it. Even if it's a slow process, you need to move toward getting all the different kinds of data that you have spread throughout your organization working together.
- Hire data scientists. It's a common problem for organizations to have too much data and too few actionable insights. The right scientist will help your company get to a place where data is working on your behalf.
- Don't forget consumer privacy. It's a hot-button issue and probably top of mind, but you need to recall that even the appearance of data abuse can cause a public relations nightmare and, worse, a feeling of betrayal among your customers.

4 The Cloud

On February 6, 2011, Mercedes-Benz USA, a long-term client of ours, became a first-time Super Bowl advertiser, when a 60-second spot starring P. Diddy and a snippet of a Janis Joplin song aired in the fourth quarter of the Green Bay Packers–Pittsburgh Steelers nail-biter. The point of the ad was to celebrate Mercedes' 125-year heritage and its action featured all the Mercedes of the world coming together to greet a new model. It was an amazing moment for a great brand, but those 60 seconds weren't the full extent of the Mercedes presence in the big game—far from it. In recent years, big-brand marketers have learned that if they want to get their money's worth from the Super Bowl—a shade under $3 million for 30 seconds and rising—then they had better create a robust program that created interest in the run-up to the big game.

To that end, Mercedes' Super Bowl campaign officially kicked off months before with a very different type of marketing idea, one that eschewed celebrities for ordinary Joes, one that activated Mercedes' fan base to build excitement around the brand and the big game. In early December, we told the world we were looking for a few good drivers who had passion for both Mercedes and social media and asked anyone who fit the bill to apply on the Mercedes Facebook page. The winners of a video contest would get a chance to compete in a very unique kind of competition: a Tweet Race. Using four specially equipped Mercedes, the driving teams would each start out in a different city and race to the site of the Super Bowl in Dallas, covering about 1,400 miles. The "fuel" for all the cars consisted not of unleaded but of tweets, a twist that turned each of the driving teams into very loud brand advocates. For every four tweets of support, the drivers earned a mile. So in addition to being good drivers, they had to gain support in social media any way they could, each building out their own community. The winner would win a 2012 C-Class Coupe.

The program was a textbook case of how creatives, strategists, and technologists can come together to engage consumers. But if you were behind the scenes like we were, you would have known the campaign was powered by an unseen force.

The cloud.

To the degree you've paid attention to the rapid growth of cloud computing, it's probably been as a way to cut costs. Although cost efficiencies are certainly one benefit, they don't tell the whole story. Increasingly, the API-enabled public cloud has empowered its users to pull off great tech and creative innovations. Mercedes' Tweet Race was a case in point.

Mercedes had decided to host the Tweet Race on Amazon Web Services (AWS) rather than the company's traditional infrastructure. That decision made all the difference in terms of cost, speed

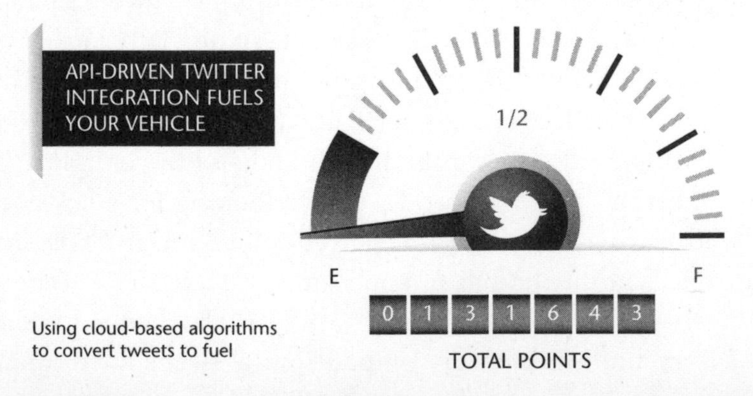

FIGURE 4.1 API-Driven Twitter Integration Fuels Your Vehicle

to market, and the innovation we could bring to bear as we ramped up interest in Mercedes' part in the big game.

Consider this:

- If we had to use a precloud infrastructure setup, we wouldn't have had the servers or the computing resources we needed for at least a month. Using Amazon, we were able to prototype and test creative ideas as early as the initial strategy meeting. We had campaign components up in four weeks that in the past would have taken six months.
- The technology that literally drove the cars was enabled through the cloud: an algorithm that tracked progress via cellular triangulation and GPS that tied into a dashboard built on an HTML5 page.
- The costs of using Amazon's servers were less than the cost of equipping the drivers with the iPads and Android devices.

In short, inexpensive, easy-to-use cloud services helped make the Mercedes Tweet Race, a complex technological solution to a marketing challenge, possible in a short time frame and at a cost much superior to traditional infrastructure. It's one small example of how the cloud offers great potential for innovation and efficiency.

We say "potential" because the reality is that many enterprises we encounter are still very skeptical when it comes to cloud computing. They've been slow to adopt, despite the successes of well-established companies, cloud advocates like Netflix, and some of the biggest disruptors in business today. Some of the reasons behind the skepticism are well placed; more often, they're not. All can be overcome.

For us at Razorfish, using the cloud is a no-brainer. Yet we're constantly met with resistance from clients and partners who would rather use their traditional data centers than faster, cheaper, and more flexible cloud solutions. Sometimes this resistance takes the shape of concerns over security or liability. Sometimes it's just about continuing to do business as usual. In all cases, an opportunity for innovation is being missed.

In this chapter, we'll argue that in a converged world, cloud computing needs to occupy a central place in your toolbox. We'll talk about what cloud computing is, explain its benefits, and examine some of the skepticism surrounding it. Finally, we'll tell you how the cloud, something you might have thought of mainly as a way of reducing costs you've accumulated from investing in traditional data centers, can help you get faster to market with better experiences for your consumers.

Grasping the Cloud

There's an old analogy, somewhat divisive in IT circles, that holds up. Your business needs electricity to run, but you wouldn't consider building your own power plant in order to get it. The same, some argue and we'd agree, is true of your company's computing resources. We're not saying this is a perfect analogy. Electricity is electricity anywhere you get it; the same isn't true of computing needs. They vary greatly from provider to provider and each provider offers a variety of different services. But the point is this: You need to think of data centers not as something you build but as something that's a service that you rent to keep your costs down, to improve speed to market, and to allow your people to focus on innovation.

This means thinking of servers as a service, not an asset. And this means embracing the cloud.

Oddly enough, one of the first important books to look at the cloud barely mentioned it. In 2008's *The Big Switch,* IT iconoclast Nicholas Carr observed that "private computer systems, built and operating by private companies, are being supplanted by services provided over a common grid—the Internet—by centralized data plants. . . . Computing is being turned into a utility."

Interestingly, the index tells us that this five-year-old book mentions the cloud by name only twice, which goes to show how far the concept has come in a short period of time. Now you can't avoid the topic, whether at tech conferences, on the cover of business magazines, or in the boardroom. And rightfully so. It's not just a technology or marketing concept. It's a fundamental business issue that touches every part of the enterprise, to say nothing of governments, nonprofits, and the online consumer experience. And cloud computing is an area of explosive growth: The analysts at Forrester have predicted that the global market for cloud computing will go from $40 billion in 2011 to more than $241 billion in 2020.

The term *cloud* means a lot of different things to a lot of different people, so once again we should begin by presenting our terms. The government has called it "a model for enabling ubiquitous, convenient, on-demand network access to a shared pool of configurable computing resources (e.g., networks, servers, storage, applications, and services) that can be rapidly provisioned and released with minimal management effort or service provider interaction."

That's a mouthful.

Our way of thinking about it is a little user-friendlier. Whereas in the past your enterprise relied on expensive-to-build-and-maintain private data centers for its hosting needs, it now uses cloud services provided by the likes of Amazon, Microsoft, Google, or Rackspace. Or at least it should be. Whereas in the past, your IT staff had to plan and budget for server capacity months and months ahead of time, it gets those resources immediately, in the time it takes to punch in a corporate credit card number. Or at least it should. Whereas in the past your company spent heavily on often underutilized server hardware, it now gets it on demand. Or at least it should.

This is the cloud: fast, cheap, powerful, scalable, and the site of intense innovation. There are three major kinds of cloud: the private, the public, and the hybrid, which combines the first two. In the private cloud, infrastructure is operated for one organization alone. This is wrongly perceived as safer than the public cloud and requires a large amount of resources to

This is the cloud: fast, cheap, powerful, scalable, and the site of intense innovation.

maintain. Furthermore, it doesn't enjoy the same economic efficiencies as hosting your storage and applications with a major public cloud provider, as we did with Amazon and the Mercedes Tweet Race. Private clouds cost more, mostly because they require more hardware and bandwidth because they aren't sharing like the public cloud does. The private cloud tends to lag behind the public when it comes to innovation, which happens first in the public cloud because that's where the opportunities are. The private cloud offerings are currently at the point that the public cloud was four to five years ago.

It is within that public cloud where enterprises can find not only efficiencies but innovation. For us, this public cloud is the cloud that matters. Its service offerings can be grouped into three major models:

- **Infrastructure as a service:** The most basic use of the cloud, this entails a provider leasing space on virtual machines, storage, and load balancers, as we did with AWS for Mercedes' Tweet Race. The magic of infrastructure as a service is that vendors have made hardware work more like software.
- **Software as a service:** More advanced, this is for customer relationship management (CRM), e-mail, and virtual desktops, and it includes anything from Google Apps, Microsoft Outlook, and Salesforce.com. What sets SaaS apart is that it's providing software or programs that don't require your organization to install software or manage physical servers in your infrastructure. For instance, you can always be running the latest software. Organizations running on salesforce.com are likely running the latest version of the software with all the latest business benefits. Ask anyone running traditional CRM software on their physical servers and they are likely one to two years behind the latest version of the software.
- **Platform as a service:** This is the future, an offering that allows you to abstract away from the complexities of hardware, whether virtual or physical, so that you can more rapidly test and develop

applications in the cloud—the entire digital application or digital experience enablement "stack." Examples are Amazon's Elastic Beanstalk, Google's AppEngine, and Microsoft's Azure.

As you can probably tell by now, at Razorfish, we've been very bullish about using cloud options, such as AWS, in place of traditional private centers. We established our cloud computing practice back in April 2010. At the same time, we became an officially designated AWS global solutions provider. This bullishness derives from a few years of coming to understand how the cloud benefits enterprises. We experienced this firsthand after we were sold by Microsoft, where Razorfish was close to its ad center and utilized hundreds of its servers. Postsale, we needed to get out of that arrangement and so began our relationship with the cloud and our relationship with Amazon.

Amazon has become the leader in cloud services for enterprises. Revenue and market share for its cloud business isn't public, but Gartner has called it a "de facto monopoly," despite all the competition it faces. And to think that just a few years ago its cloud business didn't exist.

From EC2 to the Royal Wedding

On August 25, 2006, Amazon launched a new service into public beta: Amazon Elastic Cloud Compute (Amazon's EC2). The geeky name was strange coming from the consumer-friendly company, but it did nothing to put off users. Here's how *BusinessWeek* described the moment: "Its service: cheap, raw computing power that could be tapped on demand over the Internet just like electricity. In less than five hours, hundreds of programmers, hoping to use the service to power their MySpace and Google wannabes, snapped up all the test slots. One desperate latecomer instant-messaged a $10,000 offer for a slot to a lucky winner, who declined to give it up."

Amazon at the time was a struggling remnant of the dot-com years, still best known as a bookseller that had invested in too many distribution centers. Its future was in doubt. Even the Kindle was still a year or so off. And when Amazon CEO Jeff Bezos announced that the retailer was getting into what would widely become known as cloud computing, people thought he was crazy. But Bezos and his team had years of experience under their belt and they understood that the vast collection of servers Amazon had built to deal with spikes in shopping traffic—on Black Friday, say—was largely going unused at less hectic times. What Bezos saw was that there was gold in all that underutilized capacity. After all, the world's largest enterprises suffered from the same problem. They were wasting untold millions on data centers that were provisioned for traffic that rarely, if ever, came. The difference between such enterprises and Amazon is that Bezos and CTO Werner Vogels had the vision to turn all that unused capacity into profit.

In our minds, the launch of EC2 is a convergence milestone in the Internet's disruption of business as usual, even if it might not be as obvious as the cataclysmic changes wrought by Google or Facebook. EC2 was not the birth of our era of cloud computing, but it was an important point in its maturation. It helped enterprise cloud computing grow into a powerful force that's having huge impact throughout government, culture, and, of course, business. It's already changed the way that business is done by equipping an untold number of startups with the cheap computing resources they need to get their businesses off the ground. And there's still vast untapped potential when it comes to large, established enterprises.

Since launch, Amazon EC2 has diversified its user base from just startups. There are government entities such as the U.S. Department of Agriculture and NASA Jet Propulsion Lab (JPL), which uses Amazon to process high-resolution photos to guide its robots. "At this point, JPL's data centers are filled to capacity, so we're looking for ways to cost effectively expand the computational horsepower that we have at our disposal," JPL data services manager Khawaja

Shams told the *Los Angeles Times*. "Cloud computing is giving us that opportunity."

Then there are media companies such as *Newsweek/Daily Beast* and PBS, with its more than one petabyte of streaming video each month. There are institutions such as the Harvard Medical School, which is using Amazon to host a database for genome analysis.

There are business disruptors such as Foursquare and Yelp. And, increasingly, there are large enterprises such as Virgin Atlantic and Netflix.

Pinterest, which hit 10 million monthly users faster than any site in the history of the Web, runs on a variety of Amazon services, including S3 and Elastic Cloud Compute. Between August 2011 and April 2012, Pinterest's use of Amazon's S3 grew by a factor of 10, and its use of Amazon's EC2 grew by a factor of 3. The company now has about 80 million objects stored in S3, which holds about 410 terabytes of user data.

"Imagine we were running our data center, and we had to go through a process of capacity planning and ordering and racking hardware," Pinterest engineer Ryan Park said at an Amazon Web Services Summit last year. "It wouldn't have been possible to scale fast enough."

Netflix offers probably the best example of how a big company can take to the cloud. A few years back, the great shipper and streamer of TV and movies realized that it couldn't build private data centers fast enough to handle data spikes. But Amazon Web Services, it found, could give it the scale it needed. So in 2008, Netflix stopped investing in private data centers. Instead it relies on Amazon to provide scale hosting and layers its own technologies on top of it. There have been speed bumps along the way, but Netflix has remained true to its cloud strategy, which it views as key to a future when its DVD rental business erodes and most of its revenue comes from streaming services.

The amount of traffic being served there is staggering. In 2011, Netflix was the biggest source of Web traffic in the United States, despite losing all those customers during the Qwikster crisis. Through its streaming video service, it accounts for a massive chunk of all Internet traffic in the United States, at roughly 20 percent. Consider that the next time someone tells you the cloud isn't for big enterprises.

Even some very public missteps haven't changed its path. Last June, a power outage knocked out an Availability Zone—Amazonian lingo for a subregion of servers—and triggered a problem with load balancing that caused Netflix, Instagram, Pinterest, and a host of other sites to experience significant downtime. Amazon immediately came clean, taking the blame and resolving to improve its processes. Netflix, too, was transparent about the problem. On its blog, the company identified the weak points in its infrastructure that had been singled out for improvement and even tried to use the failing as a recruitment opportunity. At the same time, Netflix executives affirmed their faith in the cloud, stating that since it made the move from a private data center approach, "We found that our overall availability over the past several years has steadily improved." In other words, despite the high-profile outage, Netflix uptime was on the whole improved since heading to the cloud.

Rock-solid relationships with companies such as Netflix has helped make Amazon the best-known and largest cloud provider. Estimates put its cloud operation at $6 billion. But it's far from the only player. Rackspace did over $1 billion in gross revenue in 2011. Salesforce is making more inroads in the cloud, as are familiar faces such as Microsoft and Google. In fact, Google's cloud services were behind one of the biggest media events of recent years.

In the early hours of April 29, 2011, tens of millions of people around the world took to the Internet to watch the wedding of Prince William and Kate Middleton. About 6 million of them stopped by the Official Royal Wedding site, where they clicked on about 15 million pages. This kind of demand would crash many sites, but the wedding site was ready. Not only did the site not collapse under the weight of that traffic, unlike BBC's video operation, which went pear-shaped for a bit—it didn't even flinch. Not bad for something that hadn't been around even a few months before—and it was all built on the cloud.

All credit goes to Google, whose Google App Engine bore all that traffic on its shoulders without so much as a slouch. Although the App Engine differs in many ways, think of it as similar to Amazon Web Services and EC2: They're both ways to host Web applications. When Clarence House—that's the official residence of the Prince of Wales—hired Google to get the site built, there was a four-week deadline. Because of App Engine and Google's infrastructure, there was no need for a massive amount of on-premises servers. Taking full advantage of the cloud, Google could apply a bunch of tools like page pregeneration and load balancing in order to ensure that it could handle all the traffic. Performance tests determined that the site could handle half a billion page views per day. On the day of the nuptials, the peak volume that Google Apps Engine processed was 2,000 page requests per second.

It all ran smoothly, as did the other 200,000 or so apps that share the Google platform and serve more than 1.5 billion views per day. Things were even busier on Google's YouTube, which peaked at 32,000 requests per second, with an additional 10,000 during the kisses.

Google celebrated on its company blog: "Whilst others were watching for a glimpse of The Dress, we were watching for a cloud platform non-event: The Google App Engine platform continued to operate normally. Both our wishes came true."

This, to our minds, sums up the benefits of the cloud: highly scalable, fast to market, and cost efficient. Institutions from Pinterest (b. 2010) to British monarchy (b. 827) are getting this. Later in this chapter, we'll discuss a lesser examined and but no less important benefit—how it spawns innovation—but before we do, let's cover the basics.

Fast, Cheap, and in Control

One of the first benefits that people want to discuss when it comes to the cloud is cost. There is the—very correct—perception that migrating your operations from private data centers to the cloud will, for the most part, result in cost reductions. Here's how.

First of all, a cloud-based approach reduces your reliance on both hardware and people to oversee them. There are no long-term investments in server capacity that you might never need. Nor is there hiring of human resources to manage it. In traditional data centers, you might need one systems administrator for every 10 or 20 servers. In the cloud, you might need one per 100 servers. And the intense amount of competition in the cloud has been good news price-wise. Last year, when Amazon dropped the prices on a number of its services, it was the nineteenth such cut in six years. Following the price cut, a small website hosted on Amazon that cost $876 per year using pay-as-you-go, on-demand pricing in 2006 would cost $250 with a contract. Meanwhile, Google and Microsoft followed suit with cuts of their own.

We're just now starting to see the impact of all this in terms of rate of ROI to enterprises. A powerful International Data Corporation (IDC) study, despite being commissioned by AWS, was conducted independently. This study found an average five-year return on investment of 626 percent and received $2.5 million per application in benefit. And this was not just for startups. The study was based on interviews with companies and institutions such as Samsung, Fox, Netflix, and the U.S. Tennis Association.

Total cost of ownership savings included development and deployment costs, which were reduced by 80 percent. Application-management costs were reduced by 52 percent and infrastructure support costs cut by 56 percent. Organizations were able to replace $1.6 million in infrastructure costs with $302,000 in Amazon Web Services (AWS) costs. The study also showed that savings increased over time. At 36 months, these organizations were seeing $3.50 in benefits for every $1 invested in AWS; at 60 months, they were realizing $8.40 for every $1 invested.

The IDC survey also addressed a second key benefit from the cloud: speed to market. AWS speeds up application development and deployment, and in some cases reduced overall developer hours needed by as much as 80 percent. AWS also allowed for faster integration of systems than did some alternatives. The customer interviewed saw more than a 500 percent improvement in efficiency throughout the software development life cycle.

"With AWS, we are able to launch some of the services instantaneously," one customer was quoted as saying. "It would take many months, if not a year or more, to build out that whole infrastructure from scratch. Estimated additional annual revenue is $2 million-plus."

IDC gave credit to Amazon's API, which reduces the amount of custom code that needs to be written. "The automated provisioning, dynamic scalability, management, and monitoring that are part of AWS mean that the development of applications can be simplified because many key services that govern application behavior no longer have to be coded; instead, they can simply be configured as part of deployment."

At Razorfish, we've found that complicated e-commerce sites that used to take six to nine months of build are now more in the neighborhood of four to six months. Using Amazon's Elastic MapReduce (EMR), which we'll discuss more later in this chapter, we've been able to get processing jobs that used to take three weeks down to just 8 hours. And you saw how fast we were up and running for Mercedes Tweet Race. That project would not have been possible, quite literally, but for the cloud.

The takeaway here is that the cloud makes things faster and cheaper. But that's not all it does. Now let's look at how it can make things better.

A Tsunami of Data

Throughout this book, we'll argue that one of best ways to create engaging and effective consumer experiences is to use data to inform them. This is easier said than done. Enterprises are still struggling to work with the tsunami of data that's washing over their organization. The cloud is shaping up as an important tool here.

Much as you've heard nonstop about cloud computing, you've probably reached a saturation point in news articles about big data. Big data have been famously defined as the point when data sets become so large that innovation is required to deal with them. And make no mistake, the data sets have gotten large. IDC projects that the digital universe will reach 30 zettabytes (ZB) by 2020.

But big data are big nothings unless you have the tools to process and yield actionable insights for your business. Clearly, great computing power will be needed to make sense of all the data. And that's where the cloud comes in.

Consider how one startup has used the cloud.

Etsy hit the scene in 2005 and quickly became a media darling as a place for hobbyists and professional artists to sell handmade or vintage items. The company, which makes money by charging a small listing fee for each item and by taking a 3.5 percent cut of every sale, has experienced heady growth. By 2007, Etsy made its one-millionth sale. By 2010, it had a valuation of $300 million. The following year it crossed the half-billion dollar threshold for sales, and by 2012 it was raising funds for a global expansion.

A *Wired* magazine article suggested that Etsy's success, even through the economic downturn, results from its focus on customization and personalization, something the Web has taught us to like. Wrote columnist Clive Thompson, "After years of molding the digital world to suit our style, is it any wonder we want to do the same to the physical realm?" A big part of that customized experience is made possible by the cloud and how Etsy uses it to make sense of large amounts of customer data created by its community.

Etsy's crafty bazaar is vast and, happily, the site provides some tools to make sense of things. One of its unique features is called the Taste Test. This allows users to sift through a bunch of items available in Etsy's marketplace. The user is asked to select several that he or she likes and, based on those preferences, the site suggests a number of product recommendations and points to other

Etsy users with similar tastes. Taste Test is a simple, elegant function that hooks you into the Etsy experience, which at first can seem overwhelming. But it rests on a serious amount of computing power. A small company such as Etsy can afford the kind of computing power to process billions of page views on a regular basis that creates these kinds of experiences because of the cloud.

Taste Test and other Etsy functionality are powered by Hadoop, an open-source platform that's become very useful to online retailers in helping them provide relevant search results to shoppers. It's especially good at processing that unstructured data that's the fastest-growing piece of big data deluge. Hadoop, which can run on different machines that don't share memory or disks, is able to process large amounts of data because it breaks that data into pieces and spreads it across servers.

"With more data and the ability to process it, companies can see more, they can learn more, they can do more," said Hadoop developer Doug Cutting to *Computerworld* in 2011. "[With Hadoop] you can start to do all sorts of analyses that just weren't practical before. You can start to look at patterns over years, over seasons, across demographics."

Hadoop, however, is not easy to use and you need a great deal of training and expertise that many companies don't yet have. Alternatively, you can use an implementation such as Amazon EMR, which removes much of the complexity, as Etsy has done. Essentially Etsy can process its data using almost exactly the same tools that Google does to the process the whole Web. This is an example of how an enterprise can use the cloud to actually shape and improve a consumer's experience with its brand. We've seen this again and again at Razorfish over the years. Serving up advertising based on the viewers' browsing history requires a good deal of data-processing power, and those requirements have only grown as more and more clients engage in targeted advertising. And then there are huge data sets that emerge from shopping-intensive periods, such as the holidays. To deal with all this, we moved away from a data center approach and used Amazon's

EMR. EMR gives us capacity as we need it, which in turn reduces close time and causes fewer delays in processing. There's no upfront investment, time, or money in hardware, and no need to add IT staff to manage it.

Approaches like this will only become more crucial as we grow more adept at working with big data. The innovation that's currently going on is going on in the cloud, not in private data centers. Companies such as Kognitio, Vertica, and Teradata Aster Data Systems are building segmentation algorithms for cluster analysis, and allow you to identify your segments. These are complex algorithms that had been relegated to academia that are now available to anyone who uses such infrastructure. We talk more about segmentation later in the chapter about data-driven experiences, but the important point for now is that all this innovation is going on in the public cloud at a fraction of the time and cost it would take in the private data center. If you're not using the public cloud, you're missing out.

Clouding the Cloud Issue

By now, the benefits of using the cloud for your infrastructure, services, and platforms should be clear. For years, we've been trying to hammer home the benefits of the cloud, presenting what we think is a case for moving at least part of your tech setup there. Yet we're constantly met with resistance from clients and partners. There are three main sticking points: security, sunk costs, and legal. Now we'll look at each issue, one by one, to help relax your concerns.

Analyst firms and technology publishers are constantly polling IT executives on their biggest concerns about cloud computing. Look at enough of them and you'll see patterns. One is that security is overwhelmingly the biggest source of anxiety among tech decision makers as they think about the cloud. Example: A survey from IDC in September 2011 discovered that less than a third of IT executives feel that the benefits of cloud computing outweigh its risks.

Nearly a quarter of the 500 executives surveyed said they don't fully understand the regulatory and compliance issues in cloud computing. Forty-seven percent said cloud services create a security threat.

This is just one of many such findings. Now try to find a quantitative examination of actual security breaches in the public cloud versus private data centers. Good luck with that. As far as we can tell, such breaches do not exist. One big challenge with that comparison is that public cloud issues are public, while private cloud administrators are typically not required to mention when they have an intrusion. When you spend some time thinking about this objectively, cloud security concerns have an urban-myth feel about them. They get passed along without real evidence or examination. Smarter CIOs are starting to realize this.

At a GigaOM conference last year, Juergen Urbanski of Deutsche Telekom's T-Systems confirmed that security was the number one cloud-related concern, but he added: "If you peel back the onion a little bit, about 90 percent of those concerns are really perception versus reality—in other words, it's evident to everyone that your money is better off in the bank, but with data, people are like 'is it really safer in the cloud?'"

Here, we would agree.

The assertion that private data centers are more secure than the public cloud is a common one, despite the absence of empirical support. It doesn't help that the cloud has been bedeviled by a few high-profile instances of hacking, including the sad story of a *Wired* reporter who had a massive chunk of his personal information wiped out by a digital ne'er-do-well. His story is a consumer cloud story, not an enterprise one, and so only partially on point, but on a perceptual level it does suggest some of the issues that cloud adoption faces.

Last August, in great detail and at great length, Mat Honan told the story of how a hacker deleted his digital life, from his child's baby pictures to his Gmail account, and sparked a lot of anticloud sentiment. Even Apple cofounder Steve Wozniak was among those screaming about the cloud's security holes. The reality, however, is that the hack had less to do with problems with the infrastructure than the fact that customer service staff at Apple and Amazon could be duped into coughing up Honan's personal information. The security takeaways were more about setting up strong passwords and making sure that your e-mail account can't be easily hacked and having a customer-service operation that won't fall victim to social engineering–based hacking attempts. If these are problems for corporate IT, well, then you need new corporate IT.

The Honan affair "wasn't a cloud security failure," wrote the blogger Rodney Brown. "It was human error, and that will keep happening whether attacks are aimed at the cloud or an on-premise IT structure—as long as businesses just pay lip service to the training and tools needed to prevent it."

One belief is that many security breaches come from the internal teams who have contact with the servers. Back in 2001, a *Network World* article said that it was as high as 80 percent. Conventional wisdom says that number has changed significantly. Either way, it seems public cloud security will have greater strength for both intrusion risks. That said, it is incumbent on the major cloud providers to keep improving security—and, given the potential growth present in enterprise migration to the cloud, they have every incentive in the world to do so. Using the cloud requires fewer internal team members to support the same number of servers. Both factors contribute to reduced risk. To sum up, security is an emotional issue that has little grounding in fact. The strongest argument impacting enterprise concerns with the cloud may be the fear of a "public" announcement. With a private cloud, security issues are a private issue, but that doesn't mean your customers' data is any safer. It is even likely that the data is less safe. For those who are still concerned, workarounds exist, such as having data hosted in the private cloud and computing in the public cloud.

The second most common point of resistance we get with migrating to the cloud is the issue of sunk costs. Many enterprises have made long-term investments in power, hardware, contracts with colocation partners, and staff to support all of this. A survey of almost

1,500 IT professionals in October 2012 revealed that the most popular barrier to cloud adoption wasn't security but sunk costs. Of those respondents who weren't on the cloud, 38.1 percent said that "they had delayed the adoption of cloud services and applications because they had already invested too much capital in internal IT infrastructure solutions." Private clouds and colocation providers have early exit penalties that could cut the benefits of moving to the cloud.

Sunk costs are an interesting economic and psychological topic that have been studied at least since the 1960s in several academic fields. Here's an example of how they work: Assume that you bought a theater ticket two weeks ago for $75. Now it's the night of the show and you don't feel like going. You have a decision to make. Like many people, you feel what's known as a loss aversion that weighs heavily in your decision-making process and you consider that sunk cost—the price of the ticket—in your process despite the fact that the cost is not retrievable. Economists would call this bit of irrational decision making the sunk-cost fallacy; you should consider only the incremental value that you'd get from your decision to attend the show or not. Either way the money has been spent; going to the show won't bring it back, and it might only make you miserable. Famous examples of the fallacy include any number of wars as well the Concorde program, developed in the 1970s despite the fact that the French and British knew early on in the process that it would be a money loser. The program wasn't wound down until 2003—27 years after the wheels first went up, strong evidence of just how powerful the sunk-cost fallacy can be.

> Deciding that you need to stick with private data centers just because you've spent a lot of money there is, at its core, irrational decision making.

Less famous instances take place all over corporate world, where IT managers hang on to old technology simply because there's been millions of dollars invested there. This, we argue, is anathema to innovation in today's world. Deciding that you need to stick with private data centers just because you've spent a lot of money there is, at its core, irrational decision making. We're hopeful that as marketers grab more control of IT budgets we'll see less of this kind of justification.

The final and probably most legitimate point of resistance concerns liability. Enterprises thinking about working with the cloud want to treat data liability as if it were a traditional data center. They usually want to be able to sue a data center for any amount if anyone messes with data. Traditional data centers will own liability because they're sitting next to the servers, as they have the superuser password. Amazon and other cloud companies, however, will have none of this.

This issue popped up a couple years ago when the relationship between Eli Lilly, an early cloud adopter, and Amazon Web Services got a bit choppy. Eli Lilly had been rather public about its use of AWS for some data-processing needs. On one occasion the company needed 25 servers to crunch a lot of data very quickly. There wasn't time, however, to go through the procurement process because it would have caused costly product delays. So Eli Lilly turned to Amazon for support. It became a case study that was often trotted out, with the CIO publicly extolling the benefits.

Then, suddenly, things soured. There were reports of a rift in the relationship. Amazon, it was reported, wouldn't accept some liability for outage and security breaches as the pharmaceutical company moved more important data sets into the cloud. There was talk of a split and, while that was never confirmed, Eli Lilly certainly has disappeared from the ranks of public Amazon boosters.

Both sides—enterprises and cloud providers—have a lot of work to do on this issue. Cloud providers, if they want to attract enterprise clients, can't live in a take-or-it-leave-it world when it comes to liability. One possible solution includes insurance options. In any event, there needs to be more adaptive thinking going on. One also needs to realize that the baby can't be thrown out with the bath water. The cloud offers too many benefits to allow legal disputes to obscure.

For those who remain skeptical of the cloud, you have to ask yourself a few questions:

> Is your website doing anything more complicated or at a scale larger than Netflix?
>
> Is it doing anything more innovative than Pinterest or Etsy or Instagram?

And, while you're at it, ask yourself this:

> Is security any more a concern for you than it is for the U.S. government?

In early 2011, the federal government adopted a cloud-first policy, meaning that all agencies needed to evaluate a cloud strategy before making investments in private data centers. It was a key initiative of the federal government's first CIO, Vivek Kundra, who explained it all in a strategy document that consists of 43 well-written pages that hold up as a strong primer on the cloud.

In the document, Kundra estimates that as much as a quarter of the federal IT budget could be migrated to the cloud. And he describes the federal government's old IT approach in a way that should resonate with many enterprises. That traditional environment, he wrote, "is characterized by low asset utilization, a fragmented demand for resources, duplicative systems, environments which are difficult to manage, and long procurement lead times."

He writes of the less than 30 percent of server utilization that typically occurs, the years it takes to get new data centers built, the burdens created by asset management and, perhaps, most provocatively, the risk-averse culture that this infrastructure setup cultivates. And he's good on specifics. When the Cash for Clunkers plan was introduced, demand was dramatically underestimated. A total of 250,000 transactions were expected in four months; within the first 90 days, almost 700,000 transactions were processed. The site, which was hosted in a traditional data center, crashed almost immediately, shining a harsh light on an infrastructure that simply wasn't good enough. The failures of Cash for Clunkers are evidence of how difficult it can be to predict demand and a reminder of how we live in a world where Amazon and Google and other players ensure that you don't have to.

Although Kundra left for the private sector and Salesforce, his program quickly began to bear fruit. An April 2012 survey of federal IT leaders found that the government was already saving $5.5 billion annually by using the cloud, with savings likely to rise to $12 billion. And even the Department of Defense, with all of its very legitimate security concerns, was taking part.

Kundra is most compelling when he describes the ultimate outcome of not moving to the cloud. He writes, "These inefficiencies negatively impact the Federal Government's ability to serve the American public."

We'd argue that those same inefficiencies are interfering with a brand's ability to serve its consumers. Yes, cost and speed are important piece of cloud computing, but it's so much more than that. Underutilization of the cloud and overutilization of private data centers ensures that companies will not be as innovative as they should be. They open the door to being outmaneuvered by startups that understand the cloud's virtues and use them to their advantage.

And what company these days can afford that?

Convergence Catalysts

- Pilot a cloud program, with our Tweet Race project as a model. Mercedes didn't shift its entire enterprise infrastructure over to Amazon, just this one-off project. Take a look for yourself at the cost savings and innovation possibilities. Create benchmarks for cost and speed, and observe how the cloud compares to your legacy infrastructure setup.
- Educate yourself. There are now more cloud-computing resources that anyone has time to read. Likewise, there are

dozens of conferences including big ones put on by Amazon and Salesforce. Conversations there will help alleviate some of the concern about the cloud if you're skeptical. Or, if you're trying to sell the cloud into your organization, they'll give you even more ammunition.

- Do a bit of daydreaming. Think about how you might be able to redeploy your IT staff if managing data centers or private cloud configurations weren't part of their job descriptions. Or how you might reallocate the budget that's supported private data centers. When talking about the cloud in your organization, remember to focus on innovation, not just cost.
- Be wary of scare stories about the cloud. Often the most hyped tales have to do with the consumer cloud, which is a whole different set of security issues that don't impact the enterprise.
- If public cloud security is still an issue for you, try a hybrid solution in which your data is in the private cloud and your processing is in the public cloud. The important thing is to understand and recognize cloud computing as a trend that in coming years will be hard to resist. At the very least, it's time to begin to understand what it can bring to your business.

Marketing Is Commerce, Commerce Is Marketing

London's Piccadilly is both the best and the worst kind of environment to try to sell luxury cars. Slicing through some upscale neighborhoods, the wide boulevard is highly trafficked by sophisticated, discerning, and affluent urban dwellers—exactly the kind of buyer that a luxury automaker is looking for. But this is London, so real estate comes at a premium, meaning that a sprawling showroom big enough to show off all of an automaker's models and derivatives probably isn't in the cards. Most don't bother to try and settle for installing showrooms in out-of-the-way parts of the city or even outside it.

Audi, however, decided to crack the code. Last year, just before the Summer Olympics, the company opened a revolutionary new showroom in Piccadilly. Audi City, designed by our Emerging Experiences Lab, takes prospective buyers through the range of possibilities by using immersive technology. Only Audi's halo cars are present in the showroom, but by using this technology a shopper can look at every model, derivative, color, and specification and virtually experience the customized car they're seeking.

Using multitouch displays, the buyer configures his or her dream ride from millions of combinations, visualizing it with photorealistic three-dimensional technology. To experience it, the shopper "tosses" the image onto a floor-to-ceiling power wall, where that dream car stands before him in life-size scale. Then the shopper can gesture to interact with the car, using Kinect technology to explore every angle.

There's also a tactile portion of the experience. After the car has been visualized, it's time to feel different materials, such as the upholstery. Indeed, many physical bits of the car are RFID-tagged so they can be applied to the configurator. And because Audi knows the purchase process doesn't necessarily begin and end in the showroom, the car shopper can take home a USB stick with the configured car and pop it into the home computer. It'll have the exact configuration that was made in the showroom.

Audi City is inarguably an amazing technological experience, but you're probably wondering, is it moving metal? In just a few months since opening sales figures have increased by more than 70 percent. Cars can be ordered at the site with the customer's local Audi dealership taking care of delivery, or they can be delivered in the Audi City handover bay. It's worked well enough that Audi is going ahead with plans to open 20 digital showrooms in major international cities by 2015. Audi Cities will be popping up all over the world, showing that you don't need to have the car on hand to sell it. And demonstrating the brand experience doesn't end at the point of transaction, a perfect example of what we call Commerce+.

One of our overarching points in this book is that brand marketing is no longer one-dimensional. It's now a two-way process, with the company and consumer in constant dialogue. A marketer must provide continuous "minibrand" interactions with its consumers and influencers. Every interaction with a consumer must be considered a brand moment, and that point at which the customer finally decides to part with his hard-earned cash is no exception. Unfortunately, many marketers have been slow to see how the transaction is a point along the customer journey that needs just as much attention as any other. When commerce is marketing and marketing is commerce, a commerce provider no longer can think only about

FIGURE 5.1 The Commerce Experience for Your Consumers Is One of Your Strongest Marketing Opportunities.

> The transaction is now the center of a cyclical and continuous brand experience.

the pure transaction. The transaction is now the center of a cyclical and continuous brand experience. Reflecting this reality, Commerce+, as we call the intersection of brand and technology, encompasses anything that enables or influences the shopping and buying experience across Web, store, mobile, and other connected devices. This includes demand generation, CRM, and progressive branded experience design for shopping and purchase, as well as consulting and implementation services for core transaction platforms.

Understanding how technology affects the buying experience is crucial, but if your understanding of the contemporary retail scene is formed only by quarterly e-commerce results, then you're missing the big picture. While e-commerce continues to grow—as we write, comScore has just announced the twelfth consecutive quarter of year-over-year growth—huge challenges loom for the biggest retailers. And we're not just talking about the untrammeled growth of Amazon, whose constant innovation should have retailers concerned. In many ways, we're in a perfect storm that's shaking up how commerce gets done.

Consider these two macro trends:

- **Customers expect more information about products before they make purchases.** A big part of this shift is the rise of the consumer voice that we described at length in Chapter Two. Prior to the rise of the social media, the consumer had no voice or mechanism to speak his or her mind. If the brand didn't live up to its promise, there wasn't a mechanism for the consumer to challenge the failure except to buy a competitive product. Social media has allowed the consumer voice to be heard and its influence can impact a brand's bottom line for both the good and the bad.
- **Customers expect a consistent experience whether in-store, online, on the phone, in-app, or wherever.** And so it follows that retailers need to use technology to create a better consumer experience. Although front-end flourishes are part of this, this isn't just about slapping up digital screens all over the store. Much work has to be done on the back-end and on the organizational chart. There's a huge fragmentation of customer data and marketing content across disparate systems and, too often, no unified view of the company's inventory, let alone its customers. This needs to be rethought. Commerce is a great arena for helping marketing to become more data-driven. For example, after we recently installed Oracle ATG recommended product technology, an e-tailer saw a lift in sales of 25 percent. The technology that enables the transactions is important (Oracle, IBM, Demandware, or Hybris), but it is more important to ensure that the transaction can provide an experience that reinforces the brand promise. If not, the brand will falter.

In this chapter, we'll examine how smart retailers are dealing with this perfect storm and how they're preparing for the future, a future that will look a lot like Audi City. We know that not every brand can afford the same kind of investment as a luxury automaker, but they can learn principles that can be applied to any brand in any category in any geography. Although Audi City is a technological marvel, it is also entirely on brand. Audi's slogan and organizational ethos are contained in the phrase *Vorsprung dur Technik,* German for "Advancement through Technology." Audi City is one articulation of that.

Fans have long expected an Audi brand experience that is technologically driven. This used to be limited to the car's advanced engineering. Now it's applied throughout the experience, including the dealership.

Other retailers have taken a similar approach, both in and out of store:

- Patagonia has launched its Common Threads Initiative, dedicated to buying and selling clothes in a more sustainable fashion. The outdoor clothing retailer opened an eBay storefront as a marketplace for secondhand clothing, an unprecedented move in retail that basically asks consumers to reduce unnecessary consumption. Regardless of what it does to the bottom line, it made emotional sense for a brand long committed to progressive causes.
- Burberry, an early fashion mover in social media, launched "shoppable videos" that merge an ad campaign with a buying experience. Viewers can buy the clothes and accessories worn by the actors simply by clicking on the item and picking a size.
- And, of course, there's Apple, whose retail model has become the business world's gold standard. A consistent experience around the world, from the tilt of the laptops to the Genius Bar to the option to get your receipt via e-mail, the Apple Store is the epitome of merging brand and commerce.

In these and other experiences, technology is used to deliver the brand wherever and whenever consumers want it and in a manner that adds value. It's not about e-commerce, m-commerce, omnichannel, or any other buzzword. It is, simply, about the consumer.

The Store Is Dead, Long Live the Store

Is there an experience more central to American consumer culture than a trip to the store? A visit to the local butcher. A soda at Woolworth's. A Friday night at the mall. A J.C. Penney white sale. The madness of a Black Friday at Walmart. Queuing up at an Apple store for the latest release. Being served up the perfect recommendation by Amazon. The history of American business can be observed through the lens of how retail has evolved, from its mom-and-pop origins, to the rise of the department stores such as Woolworth's and Wanamaker's, to the era of the mall and then the big box, to our current chaotic age in which remnants of all those previous have been mixed up in technological blender.

This is a reality where e-commerce doesn't replace the in-store experience but instead alters it profoundly. As we've seen elsewhere in the customer journey, consumers' expectations are at an all-time high. Fortunately, technology exists to help meet those expectations:

- Ubiquitous computing means that retail environments are increasingly studded with screens, displays, interactive options, and so forth.
- The point of sale, long dominated by the cash register, is set for major changes from innovators such as Square, whose iPad app, Square Register, is growing in popularity among businesses large and small, thanks to features that include inventory management and sales analytics.
- Sales associates are getting their own iPads and mobile devices to help them better interact with shoppers. For Ford, we developed an iPad app that gives salespeople the ability to quickly check inventory and ensure that a vehicle with whatever specs a buyer wants is available. There's also a video that explains SYNC (voice-activated tech), and a lane-keeping system that isn't easy to demo during a quick test drive around the neighborhood.
- Rapid innovations in mobile payments mean that consumers have more and more choices for how they want to pay.

No longer is it cash or credit only as players such as Google Wallet, Isis, Square, and PayPal battle to become the next-generation payment platform. Uptake has been slower than many would like, but midway through 2012 Gartner was predicting that mobile payments would reach about $171 billion, up from about $106 billion, year over year.

- Any number of apps are out there to make the shopping experience more fun, faster, efficient, or all of the above.

Because this is a book in large part about technology and how it intersects with marketing, you might have come into the chapter assuming we're going to write off the store and make a futurist argument that bricks and mortar will be entirely replaced by pixels. We wouldn't think of it, despite the fact that building e-commerce sites has been a part of Razorfish's history since the beginning and it's still an important part of our business. E-commerce isn't all there is to commerce, and somewhat unexpectedly, it's taken technology to help us all see that. In effect, there is no e-commerce or m-commerce. There is simply commerce, an increasingly technologically enabled process that might go on in any number of touchpoints. Ingrained in our notion of Commerce+ is the idea that the customer will ultimately decide where the transaction will happen, not the retailer.

To understand this, you need look no further than the history of e-commerce. Online shopping has existed since haphazard experiments began in the late 1970s and 1980s. In 1994, following the launch of Netscape Navigator and the beginnings of the Internet as a mass communications channel, businesses began to set up shop on the Web. In 1995, Amazon and eBay launched and the rest is history. E-commerce exploded as customers began spending more time on the Internet and realized that shopping online can be cheaper and more time efficient. Between 2002 and 2011, according to comScore, e-commerce sales almost quadrupled, from $72 million to $256 million. As we write, comScore has just announced the 12th consecutive quarter of year-over-year growth.

After almost a couple decades, you'd think that e-commerce would have relegated to the store to a secondary experience. But that hasn't been the case. Technology, contrary to some expectations, hasn't replaced the in-store experience with e-commerce—not by a long shot. Although e-commerce's growth has been heady, even through the recession, physical stores accounted for nearly 93 percent of sales of products that could also be bought online during the first quarter of 2012, according to Internet Retailer. The persistence of the in-store experience can be summed up by Walmart, for which a tiny percentage of sales is believe to be from e-commerce. People still want the in-person experience of going into a store trying on the blouse, or seeing the large-screen TV in person. The rise of mobile hasn't done much to change that either, although mobile commerce sales, at about $10 billion in 2011, were expected to double in 2012, to $20 billion.

No doubt these are heady times for a fast-emerging business and down the road there may come a time when digital shopping in whatever form fully takes the place of the in-person experience. But that day is outside the frame of reference for this book and your future planning. Right now, your focus needs to be on the commerce experience as it is now and the way it is shaping up over the next few years.

Retail's Challenges

Thanks to technological change, many tried-and-true practices that arise from the four Ps of marketing—product, price, promotion, and place—have to be thrown out the window.

- **Product:** The product now is an open book. The days when all you had to worry about was *Consumer Reports* are long gone. Customer reviews are ubiquitous and routinely impact how customers buy.
- **Pricing:** Once easy to manipulate, pricing now needs to be transparent. Obfuscation won't work, and retailers have to be ready

and willing to price-match and figure out a strategy for defeating showrooming.

- **Promotions:** In-store promotions can't just regurgitate the corporate line. They need to incorporate reviews and otherwise offer social proof of the value of the products for sale. Searching online is inherently social. More than 60 percent of users start their surfing behaviors with a Google or Bing search. Page rank algorithms depend on social to drive link strength and popularity. If your site isn't part of the conversation, folks won't be finding it with Google.
- **Place:** When it comes to place, or distribution, you have to do it all. Customers want to be able to order online and pick up in-store. They want to start a transaction on the website and finish it on the phone. They want it their way, and it's more incumbent than ever on commerce providers to give it to them.

In the past, these four Ps were determined by the brand. Now, the consumer is in control, and not only does she know what she wants but the list of demands is a long one. For most of these changes we have but one company to thank.

Amazon is the 800-pound gorilla when it comes to commerce, by far the largest single disruptive force we've seen. Back in the mid-to-late 1990s, it showed us that online shopping—mainly for books—could be a reliable and fast experience. After surviving some post-dot-com bust doldrums, Amazon has unleashed a steady stream of innovation, including Prime, the $79 a year subscription that gets you free second-day shipping and, now, access to a large selection of streamable movies and TV shows. More recently, Amazon announced same-day shipping for some metropolitan areas, perhaps erasing one of the biggest benefits of in-store shopping: immediacy. Walmart countered with a similar announcement. Unlike Amazon, which will have to set up more distribution centers in states that are less tax-friendly than the ones they're accustomed to dealing with, Walmart can simply ship items out of their stores. Walmart's approach will include higher costs from pick, pack, and ship within stores as opposed to warehouses. Most important, this lets Walmart understand consumer demand. And Google has thrown their hat into the ring of same-day shipping with Google Shopping Express.

One of Amazon's most important moves came in late 2010, when it launched the Price Check app, handing shoppers a barcode scanner and search functionality that allows them to see price comparisons, product descriptions, and product reviews while in-store. The online retailer gave consumers the tool to bring price comparisons to the store aisle and enabled them to find the best price available. A big controversy resulted when the app was promoted with a 5 percent credit on Amazon purchases, up to $5 per item, and up to three items. Although books were excluded, the promotion raised the ire of novelist Richard Russo, who published a *New York Times* op-ed piece headlined "Amazon's Jungle Logic." Although the headline tells you all you need to know, the article goes on to survey Russo's literary A-list friends about Amazon. They didn't particularly like the new Amazon app. Stephen King called it "invasive and unfair," while Scott Turow, author of *Presumed Innocent,* questioned the legal dimensions of the app. In particular, the authors were very uncomfortable with the idea of using such an app in mom-and-pop stores and harming their sales. A headline on Forbes.com went one step further: "Amazon's Price Check May Be Evil, But It's the Way of the Future."

Although Amazon, once a friendly purveyor of books, was starting to look more and more like a major disruptor, there's been no indication that the backlash has had any impact on its bottom line. A few earnings-related road bumps in 2012 had to do more with investments like Living Social and distribution; its long run of double-digit year-over-year quarterly revenue growth continued unabated. What the Price Check app did demonstrate is that the technology is here to bring full transparency to pricing and that consumers aren't shy about using it.

That's why showrooming, as the practice has been known, has become a constant subject of conversation in retail circles. comScore says about 4 in 10 shoppers check out products in-store and then buy elsewhere—especially online—for a cheaper price. As of last summer, almost half of U.S. consumers had smartphones and 58 percent of them had used the phone for store-related shopping, per a study by Deloitte. Macy's has said that 90 percent of its customers research online at least occasionally before buying in the store.

And once they begin doing that there's no turning back. Typical usage rate for in-store is 50 to 60 percent of trips, per Deloitte. Edgell Knowledge Network (EKN) and eBay Local researchers found that retailers are well aware of the problem and that 8 in 10 expected it to have a negative impact on sales during the 2012 holiday season, with an average of a 5 percent loss. Deloitte, meanwhile, found that about 5.1 percent of U.S. retail sales, about $158 billion, are influenced by mobile and predicted that this number would be 20 percent by 2016. Compare that to a projection of only $5 billion in mobile sales for 2012.

Deloitte ends up with the key insight that it's mobile influence, not mobile commerce, that retailers should be focused on. Customers have a long list of expectations and at the top is a large amount of information before they make a purchasing decision. This information-gathering process looks a lot different today than it might have just five years ago. Back then, there might have been a bit of online price shopping and surfing through some product reviews, and maybe a quick phone call to a friend or two if the purchase was large enough. Back then, retailers decided what messages would be in-store and felt safe in assuming that what they told a consumer about a product was the only thing the consumer would ever know about the product. Their signage, advertising, and point-of-purchase materials made up just about 100 percent of content a consumer would be on path to purchase.

Now the customer has access to all kinds of information, the least trusted of which may be that which the brand manager or the manufacturer decides to give him. Initial reviews research is just the beginning. The growth of mobile and social have meant that a tremendous amount of information is now at the shopper's fingertips

Now the customer has access to all kinds of information.

throughout the entire purchasing process, from the time the research begins to the in-store experience. The smartphone has been the big disruptor here.

The proliferation of Apple and Android devices that can be loaded with any number of shopping apps means that consumers can compare prices, see product reviews, and check on what their social networks know about a particular product right up until the moment of purchase. This transparency has wrought havoc on the retail world, long accustomed to having its way.

Pricing practices, especially, have been shaken up. The venerable practice of regional pricing, in which prices are adjusted based on pressures in individual markets, is made more difficult. The Internet, after all, knows no borders. The same is true of offering different prices to different customer segments. In the past, retailers could create one promotion for customers who didn't have strong buying intent without the risk of loyal or likely customers not catching wind of it. Those promotions could essentially be kept secret. Not anymore.

The consumer also expects more information from third-party sources—that's a new challenge for any retailer trying to drive unplanned purchases. They want social proof, that is, what friends and family or category experts think about product, and that's not something that most retailers are set to deliver at scale of 30,000 stock-keeping units (SKUs). Some, however, have tried. One retailer we've worked with overhauled their in-store product fact tags, adding reviews, making the product description easier to read, with bullet-pointed key product features and including the average store rating. Putting raw consumers' reviews that aren't wildly positive testimonials on the store shelf is a major step for any retailer. Surely a few sales will be lost because of a low average rating, but the payoff is a deepened relationship with the consumer in-store.

Other forward-thinking retailers are turning to their sales associates to supply shoppers with information. Nordstrom excels on its integrated front-end strategy, making plenty of digital content available to sales associates in the stores. The mobile point-of-sale

(POS) system allows associates to use past purchases as well as new recommendations to get a better picture of what the customer wants. Nordstrom, too, is big on social proof. Its e-mails will use subject lines such as "Customer Faves" and feature testimonials from consumers.

And of course each new generation of mobile apps adds functionality. As we write, the 2012 holiday shopping season is upon us and retailers are rolling out their apps. Walmart's app provides maps of stores and a virtual Black Friday circular, as well as location-aware services to help navigate the aisles. Target's offered discounts on popular toys and price matching. eBay's Red Laser, acquired in 2010, is a shopping research tool that allows you to buy items at retailers such as Toys 'R' Us and pick them up at the store. Google, although not a retailer, also got into the game by providing maps and floor plans of some department stores and malls. This is the future—and if the stores don't provide peer feedback and information that customers want and are accustomed to getting, then they'll simply get it on their own. After all, it's just a click or two away.

Toward a Single View of the Customer

We've just seen how giving consumers more product information has become an essential part of commerce. Now we're going to see how using the information that retailers already have about consumers creates better commerce experiences. This is something that retailers are still struggling with on an enterprise level. Put simply, retailers need record systems capable of delivering consistent experiences to all touchpoints. So instead of 10 promotion engines, they need a single one capable of offering discounts in social, at the cash register, online, and on mobile. There needs to be a single point of truth for pricing information and product information and unstructured content.

Enterprises have historically struggled with capturing information that the customer is sharing and then leveraging that information to create a better customer experience. Thanks to an understanding of where the retail experience is often lacking and new, constantly improving technology solutions, this challenge is improving. But there's still a lot of work to be done.

Last year, Retail Systems Research (RSR) released a benchmark report on how retailers were measuring up to the goal of omnichannel commerce.

RSR found:

- Although all the retailers it surveyed believe that the shopping experience should be consistent across all channels, only 32 percent have achieved that goal.
- Retail winners, RSR's term for top performers, demonstrate a relentless focus on the customer. All of them said they plan to consolidate the shopping experience, loyalty programs, and social and digital marketing across all channels.
- The top inhibitor for more than half of surveyed retailers is not having a single view of customers across all channels. RSR's retail winners feel more strongly than other retailers that consolidating customer data across all channels is a prerequisite to prioritizing integrated cross-channel capabilities.

These findings show how far brands have to go in really cashing in on the opportunities in omnichannel commerce. But this would come as no surprise to the many, many shoppers who are routinely frustrated by gaps in the contemporary retail experience. These manifest in many different common situations. Why, if something is sold out of the store, can't the store associate order for me online or get it from another location? Conversely, why, if something is sold out online, can't it be shipped to me from off the store shelves? Why does the website know I'm a return shopper but the sales associate doesn't? Why can't I return something I buy online in the store and vice versa?

A lot of the problems stem from back-end integration issues that have popped up over the past 10 to 15 years since the rise of e-commerce. When integration is lacking, it leads to inconsistency.

If a store wants to make a holiday promotion, it has to make a new business rule 10 times for the POS system, e-commerce engine, and mobile site. The likelihood of delivering the same experience across channels is low. There's lots of friction based on dissatisfaction on the part of the consumer who expects the store to be acting out of a single repository of knowledge and insight.

Systems integration is one of the biggest challenges facing retailers today, but it's likely that your IT department isn't going to be up to taking on the challenges. Per the RSR survey we mentioned above, a majority of retail winners indicated a greater willingness to work with outside integration partners than in the past, a reflection of their belief that the internal IT organization either doesn't have the know-how or is too burdened to take on more projects. This number shot up between 2011 (25 percent) and 2012 (56 percent). Another interesting data point from that survey follows: 37 percent more retail winners believe that the marketing function should drive the cross-channel strategy forward than do other retailers. That's a clear indication of how important that intersection of brand and commerce is for top performers. It's not enough to have the right technology in place. It has to be part of an overall strategy so that, as we've mentioned before, commerce is marketing and marketing is commerce.

Here's how enterprises are attacking these challenges:

Macy's, having decided it can't afford to have its inventory segregated between online and in-store, has announced plans to equip 292 of its more than 800 stores with backroom distribution centers, blurring the once bright line between store and warehouse and allowing the retailer to apply inventory against demand at any touchpoint. Why? Greater flexibility in managing inventory means fewer out-of-stock items on the websites. It could lead to faster, cheaper shipping, perhaps fewer markdowns, and faster turnover of inventory. The trade-off is having employees rummaging through store shelves looking for items—there are costs in time and labor.

Nordstrom, with an experience that is heavily assisted by salespeople, is replacing cash registers and wrap desks with iPads as mobile POS systems, giving its sales associates much more computing power to help them interact with consumers. Putting a customer's purchasing history in the hands of an associate while on the floor allows for a more personalized experience filled with recommendations based on the customer's personal tastes.

Less obvious to the average consumer is how enterprises are dealing with organizational challenges posed by omnichannel commerce. When e-commerce operations started sprouting up in the 1990s, they were often separated from the stores' team, creating a bifurcated commerce setup that was necessary at first but that now hampers the move toward omnichannel commerce. In many organizations, e-commerce was based far away from the headquarters, often in California, and had a very different culture. Often that e-commerce culture issued from a moment 15 years back when the intern was asked to dummy up the e-commerce site. That might have been the best way to build things initially, but it isn't the right way to move forward. We now see large retailers suffering from disjointedness.

E-commerce is no different from any other touchpoint. When it was new, the incubator model made sense. Now online is core to a retailer: While 5 to 7 percent of sales happen on the e-commerce engine, 50 percent of sales in the retail store started in the e-commerce engine. Having e-commerce as a separate silo with separate success criteria doesn't make sense anymore. Vice presidents of e-commerce have more influence on how much activity they drive to the store than they do on how much revenue they collect. The days of digital merchants and brick-and-mortar merchants failing to cooperate needs to come to an end. Enterprises need a single merchant and an infrastructure that properly deploys all the right consumer data and pushes the right messages and experience to shoppers at any touchpoint they want to use.

Nordstrom is a good example of a journey that all retailers will have to make. At Shop.org's annual conference last year, Jamie Nordstrom, president of Nordstrom Direct and great-grandson of Nordstrom's founder John Nordstrom, gave an illuminating talk about the company's move toward integration. The retailer was an early mover online, but that didn't mean it figured the experience out. The website, basically, was just a Web version of the store's catalogs and there were plenty of "disconnects," to use Nordstrom's word. The retailer then invested heavily in systems integration over the several years to get the online and in-store experience on the same page. By 2009, Nordstrom said, the company had arrived. Customers could finally shop, access inventory, and pick up from anywhere they wanted. Throughout this process, one challenge was figuring out how to bridge the cultural gap between e-commerce's "fast, cool, smart kids" and the store team's "old dumb dinosaurs." In addition to struggling with the culture clash, the integration of the channels—focused on providing a single view of inventory and of the customer, and allowing the salesperson and the customer to access any piece of merchandise any time of day from anywhere—created a challenge pertinent to who gets credit for the sale.

Attribution is a major issue for retailers as they moved from siloed organizations to seamless experiences because they often have separate P&L for e-commerce and physical stores, essentially putting the two in competition for the same consumer dollar. This is, of course, wholly antithetical to the way the consumer experiences—or wants to experience—any retailer. The consumer won't compartmentalize online experience from in-store. It's all part of one continuum. It's either there or isn't.

The fix here is both better integration of e-commerce as well as fixing key performance indicators (KPIs). If the e-commerce VP is only incentivized by online sales and there are no KPIs for sending people to the stores, there needs to be a business transformation conversation around the creation metrics to help them measure and quantify impact on stores. How to establish these KPIs is not easy, and there are problems with any solution that currently exists. There are models that give the sales channel all the credit. Thus, for an online purchase that gets picked up in the store, online gets credit. In those environments, the in-store pick-up is likely to be less than optimal. The sales associates have no incentive to give you a good customer experience, and we've even seen examples where sales associates will process a return and then sell the product out of the cash register to get credit.

Then there are retailers that use point of delivery as attribution—whoever delivers the product gets credit. In this case, if the store doesn't have the product but the website does, the associate won't make the online order for the customer because then e-commerce will get credit. Instead the associate might push a less profitable product. When it comes down to it, first-touch attribution makes no sense and neither does last-touch attribution. Clever retailers have blended attribution models where all the touchpoints that influence the sale get some credit.

Roads to Innovation

So how can large retailers, with their massive legacy infrastructure and organizational challenges, innovate? It typically won't come from huge, enterprise-level transformations. Retail is one space where the lab setup has worked well.

Nordstrom's Innovation Lab, described by its team as a "lean startup inside a *Fortune 500* company," uses human-centered design thinking and Agile and lean processes to rapid prototype potential solutions that might improve the customer experience. The preferred time frame the lab works in is one-week units. A video on the lab's website depicts the building of an app that aids customers as they buy sunglasses. The features weren't known to the team going in, so the process began with a user story map that charted out how people buy sunglasses. It quickly became clear that a central function to be included on the app was a side-by-side look at photos of the customer in different glasses to see which one looks best. Using actual shoppers at the Seattle flagship store, the team was able to work out the bugs and sniff out additional functionality in real time.

Walmart's version of this, known as @WalmartLabs, is based in San Bruno, California, exactly 1,849 miles from Bentonville, Arkansas, as a sign posted there reminds the staff of West Coast techie types. The Silicon Valley lab was built over the past few years as a way to ramp up innovation and is thus far responsible for a new semantically driven search engine called Polaris; Shopycat, a Facebook gifting app; and Goodies, a subscription service for gourmet food. In its San Jose store, Walmart is testing a service that allows shoppers to search for the exact location of a particular item, which could be a real improvement of the shopping experience in a 100,000-square-foot store.

Another interesting model is Starbucks' Digital Ventures Group, which isn't a lab per se but has some characteristics of one in that it's meant to be nimble and entrepreneurial. The group, overseen by the company's chief digital officer, is responsible for all things digital, from the Web platform, to mobile app development, to the in-house e-commerce platform and business, to its branded Wi-Fi strategy, not to mention social media and loyalty programs. As such it's a combination of IT, commerce, and marketing that touches both the back-end and the front-end, the physical and the virtual worlds.

The lesson from all of these organizations is to move fast, test and learn, and fail forward. Take winners and try to integrate them into a more holistic experience. It's not all about epochal organizational shifts, but rather smaller, continuous iterative ones. Take Starbucks' mobile in-store strategy as an example.

At one point, Starbucks had two mobile apps, one for the store card and another for a store locator. It eventually combined them into a single app that became the Starbucks mobile experience—for a time. Then came Starbucks' investment in the mobile payments startup Square, and the agreement that Square would provide debit and payment processing in several thousand Starbucks locations. This meant that customers could now pay with Square's wallet app, once again complicating the experience and essentially putting two Starbucks apps on the market. Could this cause some confusion among consumers? There's no doubt. But to not do it risked losing first-mover status. It's clear that the Starbucks strategy is to move fast, see what works, and not necessarily wait for enterprise-level shifts. By the time you read this, the strategy might well have changed again. It's okay if the first version isn't perfect or long lasting. Plus, it's clear that Starbucks mobile is paying off. In its first year of offering mobile payments, it did 26 million such payments.

The Moosejaw Model

If you don't live in Michigan or you're not into outdoor culture, then you'd be forgiven for not having heard of Moosejaw. The company started out about 20 years ago with a shop in Keego Harbor, Michigan, and since then, it's expanded its footprint modestly to places like Kansas City, Missouri, and Natick, Massachusetts. Its online growth has been less modest, however, and as an example of a multichannel retailer that gets how to integrate experience, Moosejaw's size is not representative of its reputation.

The first thing you notice about the Moosejaw experience is the irreverent attitude toward branding. On the company website, there's a section called Madness that contains customer-submitted photos, a blog, illustrations of weeping tomatoes and customer dreams, contests, giveaways, and links to social media presence. This branding approach has even been expanded to offering dating advice and a breakup service in which Moosejaw would call it quits for a boyfriend or girlfriend for you.

The fun and games, however, can distract from how seriously Moosejaw takes the customer experience. Benefitting from being a newer, smaller player, Moosejaw didn't have the big integration problems that came from hooking up separate POS, customer service, and e-commerce systems. It's built one commerce engine to serve a customer whether he's on the phone, in-store, or visiting the website. Registers are Web terminals pointed at commerce engines. Customer service reps are looking at websites pointed at commerce engine, just as in-store associates are using iPod touches. The consumer-facing website is a version of the same thing. The taxonomy and features are different for each, but they all have the same systems of record. The platform, deployed five years ago, gets call centers, POS, and online commerce to a single view of products, pricing, inventory, marketing, promotions, and customers.

Moosejaw subscribes to the increasingly popular concept of the endless aisle, the notion that not all the products a company sells need to be available in the store but they do need to be accessible from the store or through a kiosk or terminal. A Moosejaw location can hold just 4,000 to 5,000 SKUs, whereas a warehouse might have 80,000. If a customer in one store wants a product that isn't available, all he or she has to do is get one of a few associates equipped with an iPod touch to order one. It'll be shipped to the customer's home, free of charge. This sort of thing would be impossible—or at least complicated—in a siloed organization. As of last year, orders placed on Moosejaw.com are responsible for 10 percent of store sales.

The iPods carried by associates keep them out on the floor, allowing them to float among the customers and products. Moosejaw clerks are empowered to price-match from competitors, but this is less of an issue when they're constantly communicating with the customers. Not only is it harder for them to reach for their phones, but customers also come to view the clerks as a source of knowledge. Newer Moosejaw locations have half the number of payment terminals that the old ones do, and 60 percent of transactions there are done on mobile devices. Moosejaw associates are quite taken with the new technology. "The employees love the mobile POS and have dubbed it 'The Future Toaster,'" Moosejaw CEO Eoin Comerford told *Apparel*. "I'm not sure why—probably something to do with the credit card swipe slot. They like that it enables them to engage directly with customers without a bulky cash wrap getting in the way." In place of the checkout counters, Moosejaw has been considering customer engagement areas at the front of stores that are more like mini-living rooms, with easy chairs and a TV. These are places where consumers can interact and more products can be shown.

Thanks to the investment in technology and integration, Moosejaw associates know what they need to know to improve the shopping experience: prior to purchases with sizing information, wish lists, and abandoned shopping carts. They understand the lifetime customer value in real time and can do a return that's slightly beyond policy. Its loyalty program is about engagement, not just about getting you to buy more stuff. There might be a text message asking the customer to send in a photo in return for Moosejaw Madness points. On the smartly designed website, an important function is granular control of the product reviews, sorting for age and experience levels. There's also a human presence. An 800 number is front and center, not buried as on other websites, and you're greeted with the opportunity to chat with an actual person. It's a reminder that to be technologically inclined doesn't mean you have to sacrifice the humanity that made you worth engaging with in the first place. Moosejaw's twice-weekly e-mail blasts offer a tool where you can push snooze as though it were an alarm clock, giving the consumer a temporary opt-out when he or she isn't interested in receiving communications.

What we've just described is, in many ways, the coming full circle of the commerce experience that began way back in history with one-to-one relationships. Think of the sole proprietor who knew customers intimately, and when they changed behavior he had a conversation with them. Then he reflected change in buying patterns. Of course, that model didn't scale well, so retailers adopted a single-to-many concurrent approach. Ads became prominent and one-size-fits-all messaging appeared in stores. Economies of scale took hold and the customer experience, by and large, fell by the wayside. Now technology, where deployed effectively, is finally becoming an enabler of that one-to-one experience on a mass scale.

Convergence Catalysts

- Look at smaller, faster movers for inspiration. Their smaller scale means that the big boys can't easily copy them, but they can provide some inspiration for iterative improvement.

- Adopt a lab or incubator model that allows you to try out different technology solutions to improve the commerce experience. The fresh air of Silicon Valley might help with inspiration from innovation.
- It's okay if the first iteration isn't perfect. Customers will forgive you as long as they sense that you are motivated by the goal of improving their experience. Look to Starbucks' constant revision of its mobile strategy. Rather than wait to have all their ducks in a row, they're continually releasing and revising their offerings.
- Consider a blended attribution model that understands the role of various channels in a consumer's purchasing decision. Cutting corners here for the sake of simplicity will only ensure the wrong kinds of competition among your various functions.
- That single view of the customer is all important. This will often require a major technological investment, ranging from a box of tech Band-Aids to an entire re-platforming. Do whatever you need to get there before a disruptor like Moosejaw, which doesn't have all your legacy concerns, beats you to it.

Media

On July 12, 2011, the management team at Netflix probably woke up feeling rather good. In fact, most mornings probably felt that way. After all, Netflix, a survivor of the dot-com boom and bust, had single-handedly disrupted the movie rental business with its mail-order DVD business and brilliant recommendation engine that kept consumers coming back.

Things were particularly looking up on that summer day. The company's stock was trading at an all-time high, just under $300 a share, and in the week before that its streaming video service was rolled out to 43 countries, including Mexico and other markets in Central and South America and the Caribbean. The service was already an increasingly popular complement to its legacy DVD mailing business in the United States and Canada. Streaming video, in fact, was so popular and so important to Netflix's future that the company had been rethinking its organizational structure and consumer offerings, including its pricing strategy, to gear up for the digital future. The new offering would be announced that day.

A post on the company blog written by marketing executive Jessie Becker announced that Netflix was doing away with its current pricing plan, which gave customers unlimited streaming and unlimited DVDs for just $9.99 a month. In its place would be two different plans, one that offered unlimited streaming for $7.99 a month and one that offered unlimited DVDs for the same price. What once cost about $10 would now be nearly $16, a 60 percent increase. Becker also announced that in order to reorganize around the new offering, the company was splitting in two, essentially walling off its declining legacy business, DVDs, by putting it under a separate management team.

The backlash was immediate.

"To say the least," wrote Greg Heitzmann in the blog's comments section, "I am shocked and appalled at your recent behavior. It seems like yesterday we were the best of friends. You informed me with your poignant documentaries; I always laughed at your corny B horror flicks. For four years you've been the gracious receptacle of my hard-earned money, but alas, your current actions have forced me to reevaluate our relationship. Your nominal price increase, while unexpected, does not deter my loyalty. However, your mouthpiece Jessie Becker's presentation of this upcharge—as an added choice for my own benefit—insults my intelligence and reveals the breadth of your arrogance. Had I been treated like an adult and informed of these changes in a straightforward, honest manner, perhaps we could rekindle our spark. Unfortunately, this course of action is no longer available; your condescending and manipulative tone has irreparably ruined our relationship."

The final dagger was his signature: "Your ex-customer."

So who is this Greg Heitzmann? A business journalist? An influential technology analyst maybe? Some sort of social media maven? Nope, he's a University of Missouri graduate and . . . well, that's about all we know about him. Despite this anonymity, his comment, which received more than 500 Facebook likes, set the tone for the more than 12,000 other comments on the blog post. Netflix, out of the blue, was facing a populist revolt whose cries could be heard throughout Facebook and Twitter, throughout the tech blogosphere, throughout the mainstream press, and throughout the stock markets, as Netflix shares began a long plummet. Yet that was just the beginning of the pain.

Two months later, Netflix's crisis deepened when the company once again took to its blog. This one was from Reed Hastings, who offered up an apology for how the first announcement was handled and then revealed that the strategy would remain unchanged. The new DVD business would be called Qwikster and customers would be required to set up and maintain two different accounts, one for DVDs and one for streaming. Customers used to going to Netflix to set their rental queue would now be sent to Qwikster.com. Wrote Hastings, "A negative of the renaming and separation is that the Qwikster.com and Netflix.com websites will not be integrated. So if you subscribe to both services, and if you need to change your credit card or e-mail address, you would need to do it in two places. Similarly, if you rate or review a movie on Qwikster, it doesn't show up on Netflix, and vice versa."

You can probably guess what the reaction was. This time the top comment was from Zachary Keith Oden: "Qwikster is lame. The name is lame. The idea behind the name is lame. Dial-up lame. What a terrible, terrible name. It brings up connotations of that chocolate bunny drink that you would valiantly attempt to pour into an ice-cold glass of milk, only to watch the powdered coco-crystals coagulate and spin in a whirlwind of sadness in front of you, all while that smart-assed bunny cackled at your misfortune. How many times would you fall prey to the Qwikster Bunny before opting for a ready-made Yoo-Hoo? How many times?"

This comment, tops among almost 28,000, received more than 1,000 likes. Like Heitzmann's, it set a tone of slightly absurdist outrage that was only heightened when it came to be known that the Twitter feed for Qwikster was already owned by one Jason Castillo, a profane high-school kid whose avatar featured the puppet Elmo smoking marijuana. By mid-October, Hastings announced that the company had killed off Qwikster, but the damage was already done.

Netflix lost 800,000 subscribers and 77 percent of its market value in four months. There was even a *Saturday Night Live* parody of the crisis to enshrine the moment in pop culture history. A year after the crisis began, Netflix had lost about two-thirds of its value and the company was still apologizing for the moves.

How did a tech-savvy, gold-plated brand that had navigated the digital age so well go so wrong so fast?

There were two key—and catastrophic—missteps that led to this disaster. First, Netflix's leadership put its organizational chart ahead of its long-loyal customers, trashing Netflix's simple and effective experience by complicating how consumers use the service and how they're billed in one fell swoop. An elegant, intuitive interface that had become essential to a lot of people was suddenly gone. Second, Netflix's leadership forgot that consumers in today's media world have their own voice and they know how to use it. This fact has been clear for some time. Back in 1999, Rick Levine, Christopher Locke, Doc Searls, and David Weinberger laid it out in *The Cluetrain Manifesto,* the well-known compilation of theses about how the Internet would change business:

> Business-as-usual . . . continues to conceptualize markets as distant abstractions—battlefields, targets, demographics—and the Net as simply another conduit down which companies can broadcast messages. But the Net isn't a conduit, a pipeline, or another television channel. The Net invites your customers in to talk, to laugh with each other, and to learn from each other. Connected, they reclaim their voice in the market, but this time with more reach and wider influence than ever.

The Cluetrain Manifesto, which still resonates today, was written before the rise of blogging and large-scale social platforms that have made it brutally easy for customers to voice their pleasures and pain. It used to be that you'd call an 800 number or write a letter or send an e-mail when you were dissatisfied. Now you just go to Twitter and fire off an angry @reply or mosey over to the brand's Facebook page and deposit your comment. Unlike the old ways of voicing your complaints, these Tweets and comments are public, viewable by other customers and the media. They are parts of a larger conversation about your brand over which you have little to no control.

Relatively few brands have responded well to this reality, though. Too many spend most of their time constructing messages that will miss consumers or fall flat in the market. They remain chained to old media models and one-way communications approaches. They see social media not as places to converse but another box into which they shove their brand message. They fail to see the many ways in which marketing has become dialogue spoken by many, many stakeholders.

In this chapter, we're going to discuss how media has changed and how smart brands are dealing with the demands brought on by this change. If Netflix is our cautionary tale, then brands like Mercedes-Benz, Coca-Cola, and Chipotle will be our inspirations as enterprises that have shrugged off old habits. We'll see that thriving in a converged media environment requires a rethink of how a brand buys media and reimagines itself as a creator of media.

It's all in the service of one goal: reaching a consumer who has become increasingly fickle about all things, not least the media she consumes.

How the Fickle Consumer Uses Media

Consumers have come to expect a lot from their commercial experiences. You might even say we've become a bit spoiled. The comedian Louis CK has a great bit on YouTube called, "Everything's amazing and nobody's happy." In his trademark acerbic fashion, he calls out people for taking technology for granted and too readily getting perturbed when everything is not perfect. Some of his ire is aimed at people who complain incessantly about the commercial airline experience: "They're like it was the worst day of my life. First of all we didn't board for 20 minutes. . . and then we get on the plane and they made us sit there on the runway for 40 minutes. We had to sit there. Oh really, what happened next? Did you fly through the air incredibly like a bird? Did you partake in the miracle of human flight, you non-contributing zero? Wow, you're flying! It's amazing! Everybody on every plane should just constantly be going, oh my God, wow you're flying, you're sitting in a chair in the sky but it doesn't go back a lot." As marketers, we don't totally agree with Louis. We should strive to perfect our experience for consumers, who have the right to demand that perfection. But he is on to something.

More and more is demanded of brands, thanks in no small part to relentless innovation in the technology space over the past two decades. Innovation cycles are faster and shorter. Great tech is less and less expensive. With each iteration of a new computer or mobile phone, the stakes are raised not just for the gadget maker but for everyone who creates a consumer experience: airlines, retailers, auto dealers, and so on.

"There's a reason why smartphones fly off the shelves," said Steve Cannon, CEO of Mercedes-Benz USA. "They add tremendous value. What we have found in our business is that these devices drive a level of expectation that consumers take with them everywhere they go. We live in an era of heightened expectation. Either you deliver on those or you don't."

Considering where Cannon is coming from, this is an incredible statement. Essentially, an increasingly ubiquitous device that costs a few hundred dollars is setting the bar for purchases that cost many tens of thousands of dollars. In other words, putting a vast amount of computing power in a beautifully designed device that fits right in the pocket has raised expectations beyond just the realm of consumer electronics.

To fail to meet those expectations is to suffer dire consequences. Loyalties shift easily in a time of so much product choice. Think about it in terms of Netflix. Streaming movies and TV shows is a relatively new thing. Yet there's already vicious competition among Netflix, Amazon, Apple, Microsoft, HBO, VUDU, and Crackle, to name just a few. The story is the same in the physical world. At your typical supermarket, the average number of items sold exploded from about 10,000 in 1977 to more than 38,000 today, according to the Food Marketing Institute. In the 1980s, it was normal for a supermarket to have three different SKUs for apples; today the average grocery store has close to 30. Department stores tell a similar story. In 2011, Walmart reversed course on a SKU rationalization program that in addition to reducing product clutter on store shelves led to a same-store sales decline. In the average store, Walmart headquarters (in Bentonville, Arkansas) had to add back 8,500 SKUs, many of which were slapped with a promotional sign, "It's back." Overall, SKUs would go up by 11 percent. If this is what's going at the world's largest retailer, then you know there are very few areas where consumers don't have some degree of choice.

This is even more exaggerated in the media world. A few decades ago, there were three TV networks, a handful of national newspapers, and a lot of radio stations. Now, all of these are available, plus a proliferation of cable TV and digital channels that grow by legions on a weekly basis. We have entered the era of big media, which, like its cousin, big data, requires innovation to handle the sheer volume of media. Now we need RSS readers, social media curators, and Google Alerts. We need technology platforms that help with curation and discovery, such as Pulse and Flipboard, apps that have become crucial tools for dealing with the content fire hose we face down every day.

For the most part, media planning and buying has failed to keep up with the rapid pace of changes impacting how consumers use media. In fact, media spending typically trails consumer behavior, a symptom of the risk-averse marketing world. To see this, look at the analyst Mary Meeker's comparison of consumer time spent with different media with the amount of advertising in each. Although it'd be wrongheaded to follow Meeker's analysis down to the percent, her work is useful as a directional guide as to how the priorities of advertising line up with the behavior of consumers. The biggest gaps between time spent and ad time show the most opportunities for correction.

In fact, media spending typically trails consumer behavior, a symptom of the risk-averse marketing world.

The smallest differentials are in television, where time spent is 43 percent and advertising is 42 percent, and the Internet (26 percent, 22 percent). The biggest gaps are in print, which gathers 25 percent of advertising budgets despite having only 7 percent of time spent, and mobile, which has 1 percent of ad budgets and 10 percent of time spent. When it comes to mobile, other companies have confirmed this gap. The research firm Marketing Evolution last year found that 1 percent of advertising budgets were going to mobile when the number should have been more like 7 percent, a figure that should jump up to about 10 percent over the next four years. The firm broke out advertising mobile activity by category and couldn't even find enough to justify location-based campaigns as its own category, another suggestion of how little innovation is going on there. Four years after the debut of the iPhone, this is an appalling indicator of where mobile innovation is.

It's worth noting that the jury is still out on the effectiveness of mobile advertising and there's a healthy debate ongoing over whether the investment on those smaller screens should be more about utility or interruption or some combination of the two. Either way, lots of brands are still struggling to figure out how to engage with consumers on mobile devices. For instance, Deloitte, setting a low bar that few still manage to clear, has found that only 20 percent of apps have been downloaded more than 1,000 times.

The point here is that media budgets are often far behind consumer behavior. All we have to do to see mobile's grip on consumers is take a look around. On the subway, commuters' eyes that were once glued to newspapers are now trained on their iPads. In malls, shoppers are fixated on their iPhones or Android devices, looking for the latest deal. This doesn't necessarily mean those devices should be bombarded with ads, but there should be more experimentation there to understand what's going. Maybe advertising isn't the optimal format for mobile, but we can't know until we try, and that will require more than 1 percent of budgets.

One of the culprits is a reliance on market-mix modeling that doesn't account well for new media channels where the level of spending is dwarfed by that in traditional media. Within these models, it's difficult or impossible for the new spending to show its worth. To generalize, these kinds of tools are more valuable for their evaluative capabilities than their predictive one. And that's especially the case when it comes to new media. There is no guarantee that the media innovation, which often exists at the level of an experiment, is being used, for lack of a better term, properly. In many organizations and for many new media channels, it takes time for best practices to emerge from testing and learning.

Another problem is media planning cycles that are too slow to react to the often abrupt changes in consumer behavior. In the digital age, it doesn't take decades for media to rise and fall—it can happen in a quarter or two.

Here's an example: Going into November 2010, people were spending more time on portals than on social networks by a small margin of a few minutes per day. Within a month, according to comScore, this had changed so that people were spending equal amounts in each. Within a year, social networks had surged ahead, while portals had declined. Thanks to the hockey stick–shape growth that happens with a hot new and inherently viral social program, sea changes occur in a matter of months, not years. Digital platforms that didn't exist during your planning session can suddenly be central to your business.

Consider how quickly the loss of the most important reference of social traffic to retailers changed. In the first quarter of 2011, Facebook was tops, supplying 88 percent of traffic. Pinterest was at just 1 percent. Within a year, Facebook had dropped to 60 percent, while Pinterest had surged to 26 percent. If you run an e-commerce site, this news is huge. Suddenly, you have a major new player that might have not even been on your radar when you were doing your annual planning. And it works the other way as well. MySpace famously lost half its traffic in a year, and 14 percent in a month. More than a few newspapers saw quarterly double-digit declines during the worst of the recessions.

Being able to respond to these sorts of changes in real time is not easy for enterprises used to buying large amounts of media well ahead of time and trained to leave little in reserve. It's a long-established mentality in which media is planned and bought many months ahead of time, an approach that once worked fine, but now in the digital age is positively antique.

To see it in action, let's look at its most exaggerated manifestation, the upfronts.

The Upfronts

During the third week of May each year, the broadcast networks announce the shows that will populate the upcoming fall season, rolling them out in the glitzy fashion you'd expect from the entertainment industry. Last year's NBC presentation saw Jimmy Fallon and Tina Fey previewing the lineup, with the casts of *30 Rock, The Office,* and others doing musical versions of their shows and *Meet the Press* host David Gregory belting out a show tune. After the drama comes the deal making, weeks of intense negotiations in which billions of dollars of advertising are spent and the ad industry's largest single market is shaped. Along the way there's plenty of speculation about just what prices the networks will get for their fare. When talking about price hikes for TV, it isn't a question of if but of how much.

For those individuals who spend most of their marketing budget in digital channels, the upfront is a striking outlier from the rest of marketing reality. Marketing in the twenty-first century is all about speed, accountability, data, and digital. The upfronts are about long-term thinking, guesstimations on the potential success of new programming, personalities, and, of course, golf.

If the upfronts sound like something ripped out of an episode of *Mad Men,* that's because it goes back to those days. The institution's history goes back to the early days of television—the very early days—when the negotiations were pegged to the TV studio's development cycle and finished up in February. In 1962, ABC made the landmark decision of setting a premiere date for its shows during a week in the fall, creating the broadcast season and buying process that has stayed with us for decades. The model went unchallenged until 1976, when J. Walter Thompson (JWT) staged a boycott of the upfronts. Displeased by steep, 25 percent cost per mille (CPM) increases, JWT sat out the talks and put all its clients into the scatter market that's sold closer to the actual air date and not sold upfront. The CPM rates were even higher there, however, and the inventory was less desirable. All the good stuff was sold out. For some time, resisting the upfronts was synonymous with disaster.

This pretty much illustrates the very seller-friendly economics of TV. Back in those days, there was a very limited supply of inventory, especially when you look at it with 2013 glasses and compare it with the vast expanses of the Internet clamoring for ad dollars, and there was great demand for it. In choosing not to commit its dollars upfront, JWT in 1976 severely limited its options. There was print, radio, out-of-home, and not much else. Cable TV didn't exist yet.

Interestingly, the intense media fragmentation that began in the 1980s and continues today hasn't done much to undermine either the economics of TV or marketing's reliance on scale buying and long-term planning. The first wave of this fragmentation was at the hands of the cable industry, which by the end of the 1970s counted about 16 million households as subscribers. Deregulation in 1984 led to vast infrastructure building and programming development. By the end of the decade, nearly 53 million households subscribed to cable, and cable program networks had increased from 28 in 1980 to 79 by 1989. By the spring of 1998, the number of national cable video networks had grown to 171. By 2002, about 280 nationally delivered cable networks were available, with that number growing steadily.

Naturally, the TV-watching audience, already a large percentage of the population before cable, didn't grow with the increase in options. That meant that attention was divided dramatically among all the programming, leaving TV with fewer individual programs that brought in truly mass audiences. In 1952–1953, *I Love Lucy* garnered a 67.3 rating, capturing more than two-thirds of the TV-viewing public as measured by Nielsen. In that decade there were two other shows that received more than a 40 percent share—*The $64,000 Question* and *Gunsmoke*. It's been downhill since then. In the 1970s and 1980s, must-watch TV like *All in the Family* and

The Cosby Show could be counted on to bring in 30-share audiences. But when Cliff Huxtable turned in his sweaters, that was it for regular programming that might capture anything close to one-third of the nation's TV watchers. While Super Bowls continue to shatter records, the average audience for prime-time fare is dwindling. In 2011, *American Idol* topped the list with an 8.1 share of viewers older than two years. In 2007, the average household tuned in to only 16 channels of the 118 channels available, according to Nielsen estimates.

You might think that CPM rates would have decreased during this time period, right?

Wrong.

Between 1980 and 2011, network prime-time CPMs more than quadrupled, from $4.80 to $22.24, according to *Media Life Magazine* (http://www.medialifemagazine.com/fact-tv-cpms-have-soared-over-the-years). Over that same period of time, the average price of a gallon of gas only increased from $1.19 to about $3. Looked at in the short term, growth rates can far outpace inflation: From 2000 to 2005, inflation grew 13.4 percent but the network was up 50 percent and spot TV CPMs grew 35 percent.

In recent years, TV sellers have continued to see steep increases. Here's how Jack Poor, vice president of strategic planning at the trade association TVB, explained it to *Media Life Magazine* (June 15, 2011): "The scarcity of network rating points has actually driven network CPM growth as demand has outgrown supply. Based on the double-digit increases achieved by the networks in this year's upfront, it looks like spot TV's cost efficiency advantage versus network will continue well into 2012."

Not a bad business, huh? Deliver fewer programs that can be counted on to attract a lot of eyes and continue to increase your rates. The constant in all this unrelenting demand on the part of advertisers for TV is the feeling that TV is still generally the best game in town for a certain kind of marketer.

That may be true, but there's growing evidence that there needs to be a better way to buy access to TV. We are starting to see more resistance to the upfront as its been conducted, although this has been less about the economics and more about how that upfront schedule fails to align with business plans. In 2006, Johnson & Johnson, a client of ours, sat out the upfronts to better align its ad spending with its business-planning cycles. Coke and Bridgestone joined them. More recently, in 2012, GM, under now-deposed CMO Joel Ewanick, balked, demanding CPM rollbacks of up to 20 percent and pulling out of the Super Bowl.

There have been more and more calls for reform from the heads of media agencies, the companies charged with actually putting the majority of advertising budgets into the market. Bill Koenigsberg, CEO of Horizon Media, has taken up the cause that the upfronts, while still useful, need to be reengineered to better align with the business needs of marketers. That would mean holding them in mid-September, not May, a switch that would cause a cascade of changes for programmers, whose new season would be backed up to January. He told *Ad Age:* "To commit in May or June six to eight months out, in terms of clients already knowing what their marketing position is going to be and what their true fall year planning is going to be, is quite premature. . . . Basically, what's broken is that decisions are being made much more in a vacuum and with less business intelligence."

Dave Ehlers, CEO of Optimedia, wants "more flexibility," including guarantees that investments could be shifted around among the assets of a major media company based on new programming and marketing opportunities as they arise. This would require setting aside invested money within the network, not holding a portion of budgets back and putting it at the risk of getting "swept." Bill Tucker, CEO of MediaVest, wants to be able to buy more finely tuned audiences, not 25- to 54-year-old women, a demographic so broad as to be useless. (Both MediaVest and Optimedia are owned by Publicis Groupe, also Razorfish's parent company.)

What we're seeing here is increasing dissatisfaction with an important aspect of the upfronts: general failure to align with the planning and business-intelligence needs of the organizations that are spending all the money. Media planning and buying need to be less about the media outlet and more about the marketer.

Just Because It's Digital Doesn't Mean It's Fast

So now you're probably expecting us, a couple of digital guys, to tell you that the remedy to all this slowness is to, well, go digital.

Yes and no.

The simple truth is this: Just because it's digital doesn't mean it's fast. Although digital has made great speed to market possible, marketers, agencies, and publishers constantly step on their own toes when trying to figure out how to take advantage of that speed. The long, slow processes that grew up over decades of mass marketing didn't go away when the Internet came to be a force. Indeed, the central point of this book is that enterprises need to reshape themselves to be faster and, in many cases, that goes for digital marketing organizations and publishers as well.

There was a great example of this in 2012 when a local newspaper in North Dakota saw its traffic explode after Gawker Media linked to give its food columnist's review of the local Olive Garden. In a matter of days, the article had more than one million views, which would have put it in on par with some of Gawker's most popular posts of the year. Despite the best efforts of the newspaper, the newfound audience was very difficult to convert to revenue. There was a bit of a bump from remnant ad sales and some attempts to cash in via an eBook and T-shirt, but none of that really panned out.

"Hits don't always lead to revenue," Jonah Peretti told *Ad Age* in a follow-up story about the difficulty of translating virality to revenue. "It's a paradox of online publishing that the moments that generate the most excitement and traffic usually yield the lowest ad rates or go unsold."

The inability of brands to get themselves near content that is both popular and engaging is evidence of how even the digital world can be quite slow in responding to the zeitgeist. In fact, part of that world is simply walking in the footprints of TV. As of last spring, there were at least a dozen digital ad sellers conducting their own versions of the upfronts, some with the same TV-esque pomp. Our sister agency Digitas has joined with Hulu, Yahoo!, YouTube, Microsoft, and AOL for the Digital Content Newfronts, where they promote high-quality video content on those websites and try to convince advertisers that they should buy in ahead of time. We like this idea as a way for channels that have invested heavily in strong original content to get their message out, no easy feat amid the din of today's media world. But it seems unlikely that this is the model that will win out for digital advertising.

As we write, the big tension in digital advertising is between programmatic and native advertising, which is in part a conversation about speed. Native advertising, to some degree a new and longer way of saying "advertorial," is about ads that are, essentially, part of the content. Native is a response to the banner ad, the much-maligned format that goes back to the Web's early days. These days there's a high degree of skepticism that consumers are actually seeing those banners that sit courteously off to the side of the content. There's a feeling that display advertising needs to be more in the consumer's face and less conspicuously an ad. Creating native ad programs requires a fair amount of planning and conversation among the brand, the agency, and publisher, which will likely be asked to do things design-wise that it hasn't done before. These programs are often one-off and publisher-specific, meaning they don't scale terribly well.

Nor are they deployable in real time as much programmatic advertising is. In programmatic advertising, media buys are automated and placed through digital platforms such as exchanges, trading desks, and demand-side platforms (DSPs). Data is king in the programmatic approach because ads are matched to consumers based on what they're likely to buy, not to Web publishers. So the media brand takes a back seat to other considerations, like what a particular consumer might be likely to buy and where he or she is in the purchase funnel. This turns the tables on the long-held notion that ads should be matched in a contextual fashion—that banners or preroll, for instance, for the latest Dell model would be best found on an electronics blog.

Programmatic media is in many ways the antithesis of the upfront mind-set, in which, whether offline or online, there's concern about the kind of content that the ad sits next to and the consumers, as constructed in so-large-as-to-be-just-about-useless demographic segments. Programmatic advertising is about finding the right customer at the right time with less regard for which situation he or she is looking. And it can be done in real time. Where the upfront is six to eight months out and driven by tradition and human interaction and scarcity, real-time bidding (RTB) is new, automated, and, true to its name, real time. This approach is growing in popularity with marketers and agencies, with RTB expected to be responsible for more than a quarter of the online display ad market by 2015. Between 2010 and 2011, Razorfish more than tripled the number of real-time impressions it purchased and, on average, saw performance improvements of more than 40 percent for our clients. The real-time nature of digital data has simply changed the way we buy media. Those who are able to understand data and act on it immediately—in real time—have a strategic advantage over their competitors. Agencies that are well versed in bid-management systems and that invest in the tools and processes to manage those systems will become industry leaders.

That growth of RTB is a useful metaphor for how media planning and buying more broadly can become nimble. We're not predicting here that the TV market is suddenly going to support RTB—although it is fun to imagine what the Super Bowl might be like if at least some of its inventory were turned over to real time. What if the fourth quarter, during which time the size of the actual viewing audience hinges on how close the game is, were open to real-time bidding and dynamic placement of ads?

Thus far TV has rejected the most dramatic attempts to modernize its market like it was a bad kidney. Last year, Google, never easy to beat back, became the latest company to give up attempts to convince advertisers to move to more of an exchange model and shut down its TV ad sales operation. Basically, the networks won't allow any programming inventory to be sold on these exchanges.

We believe that over time it will be more and more difficult for TV's content providers to hold this position. Television will become more and more like the Web as more TVs are connected to the Internet and as set-top boxes get more sophisticated and deliver more usable data on who's watching what. TV ads will eventually become more data-driven, with better targeting and dynamically served. We're already seeing some signs of this. Allstate last year ran an ad for its renters' insurance product across Dish Network and DIRECTV and it only appeared on the screens of subscribers who weren't homeowners.

In the meantime, there's plenty of room for media plans to smarten up and become more responsive and import a little of the Internet generation's test-and-learn philosophies into an older medium. Shaking off the organizational torpor that has come from decades of straightforward media strategies isn't impossible.

Let's look at some brands that have already done this.

Imagining Brands as Publishers

One of the best examples comes from Chipotle, the chain of burrito restaurants. Last year, its "Back to the Start" campaign racked up tons of consumer engagement and industry awards with an animation pointing to Chipotle's support of sustainable agricultural techniques. The video featured Willie Nelson covering Coldplay's "The Scientist" and depicted a farmer having a crisis of conscience over inhumane processes. Shortly after it was posted online in August 2011, the video took off, garnering millions of views fairly quickly. The next month it began to appear in more than 5,000 movie theaters.

Chipotle, realizing it had a hit on its hands, had to rethink its rather modest media plan. Originally, there were no plans to air the ad on TV, in part because TV advertising is not what Chipotle does. The brand grew to prominence based on word of mouth and some irreverent but small-budget campaigns. Its ambivalence about advertising could be seen in its tricky relationships with ad agencies. It went through four in five years (as reported in *Advertising Age*, September 29, 2011). But once the brand's management saw how "Back to the Start" was resonating with consumers, they decided to take a chance on a big stage and bought air time on the Grammy Awards last February. Being a newbie didn't mean that Chipotle was going to cheap out a 30-second version of the ad. In its first-ever national ad buy, they ran the whole 2-minute video, a very unconventional move for anyone, let alone for a marketer with a lean media budget. It worked, though, with any number of news outlets saying that the Chipotle and Willie Nelson's beautifully quavering cover sold the show. Wrote a *Time* magazine critic, "The most enjoyable musical thing I saw last night was not a live performance at all. It was a Chipotle ad."

Not long ago this media strategy would have been unthinkable. TV ads were always given a big reveal and were rarely leaked out ahead of time. If they were tested, it was in controlled focus groups, not in the wilds of YouTube. The beauty of the Chipotle program was that it was essentially a media plan designed in an iterative fashion with feedback from consumers built in. It featured a just-in-time media approach that got Chipotle huge bang for its buck.

This approach isn't possible when all you're worried about is buying as much media as you can for the lowest prices you can as far in advance as you can. We're not advocating that every media plan go this way and, to be fair, some of Chipotle's success has to be attributed to serendipity. However, there is a clear lesson in the benefits of test and learn and leaving yourself budget for on-the-fly changes. Although the advertising business rarely uses it, there is a middle ground between the polar extremes of upfront buying and real-time bidding.

Another way to think about media is to step out of the campaign-based mentality and begin thinking of your marketing as something that's always on. Traditionally, marketers have structured brand communications almost wholly around their own business calendar of launches and promotions. But the reality that's incredibly clear in the Internet age is that consumers don't work off your calendar. The business of maintaining a brand is a 24/7, 365-day-a-year process. Sure, there will be periods of both heavier activity and lulls, but the consumer experience has to be managed at all times. Social media is especially useful for this, because, with effective community management, those followings can be reached cheaply, quickly, and regularly without the expense of ad campaigns.

But some marketers are making even bigger bets. Red Bull's media house makes high-production-value–branded content, like *The Art of Flight* documentary, for which it charged $10 a download on iTunes, expecting it to pay off. Coca-Cola, perhaps feeling the heat from the energy-drink maker, last year reimagined its corporate website as an online magazine called *Journey*, named after a publication distributed to Coke employees between 1987 and 1997. The first redesign in seven years helped to turn Coke into a publisher, with its digital and social media team "re-formed in the last year to look more like an editorial team at a long-lead magazine . . . with a production schedule and an editorial calendar," as director Ashley Brown told the *New York Times*. Brown added: "We are acting as newshounds in the organization. It's very much like at a newspaper or a magazine."

These kinds of moves, trading out your boring corporate site that rarely changes for a dynamic content vehicle, represent a tectonic change for marketers.

"We're shifting from an old model to a new one," said Steve Cannon, CEO of Mercedes-Benz USA. "In the old model, it was about big campaigns, big dollars, and pushing a few campaigns into the market over the course of time. Now there's new outlets that have us in a constant publishing mode. It's about nonstop content creation where storytelling possibilities are multiplying. You can't feed a social channel with one campaign every six months. If you do, you're irrelevant."

For Daimler's eco-friendly Smart cars, we came up with Humor the Haters, an always-on social program in which the Smart car team responds to the misinformation surrounding the diminutive vehicle—that it's too small or fragile or wimpy—with good-natured wit. Most brands would just ignore a tweet like this one: "Saw a bird had crapped on a Smart Car. Totaled it." Or, when they do react, they get overly serious. We, however, came back at it with some humor, creating an infographic that depicted how much bird crap it would actually take to knock out Smart's Tridion Safety Cell. The tweet was picked up by a number of media outlets and generated more than 5 million impressions, turning a simple joke at the brand's expense into a publicity opportunity. It was featured on Reddit, Buzzfeed, the Daily Mail, CBC News, and CNN. As a result of the program, brand mentions increased 61 percent week over week and positive sentiment grew from 26 to 33 percent, while negative dropped from 16 percent to 14 percent.

How does this sort of strategy fit within the overall media plan? For Cannon, there's a clear sacrifice that will resonate with many marketers. In the postrecession marketing business, it's rare to find corporate largesse with which to sponsor experimentation in new and tough-to-measure media channels. Media spending has become a zero-sum game of sorts, in which spending on new kinds of content in new channels means pulling back on the old ones. "If I'm going to break off money from overall budget," Cannon said, "that means I'm going to do fewer commercials in my traditional space against my traditional customer who I already know is in my consumption wheelhouse."

What's crucial—and should be copied by marketers of all kinds—is Cannon's line of thinking. There's every reason in the world for MB to do things as it always has when it comes to its media mix. Mercedes has a built-in excuse to justify being anti-innovation tendencies: its core customer is an older demographic not known for fast-changing media habits. It'd be easy enough to let other brands with younger-skewing buyers figure out the social space. Cannon, however, has rejected this line of thinking.

"We could have played fast followers," he continued. "If we were a finance-driven company, we could have asked what's the ROI given that our average customer is around 50 years old?

We could have said, for us to reach out Gen Yers makes no sense, so let others do it and we'll learn. However, rapid development of digital and social media obliged us to jump into the fray. You can't risk being late. You can't let competitors build mass and connections to a generation while you're watching. That led us to make a disproportionate investment compared to what our demographic would justify."

This is the kind of perspective that's necessary when it comes to media planning in today's world. Rather than base all his decision making on near terms, Cannon is thinking ahead of the game. He's focused on institutional learning and figuring out a new space and engaging with a set of customers despite the fact that they don't have—and aren't supposed to have—Mercedes in their consideration set—yet. (It is worth noting that as we spoke, Mercedes-Benz was preparing for the 2013 launch of its CLA-class, a sports sedan meant to appeal to a younger demographic as a new entry point to Mercedes-Benz.)

Asked if his change in media strategy has worked, Cannon points to his brand's growing presence on Facebook and Twitter.

"The engagement level is high," he said. Then anticipating an objection that we didn't make, he added, "You can't measure direct effects of a commercial either. I absolutely believe engagement level with a brand is not a soft metric but a hard one. I'll take that over CPMs all day long."

In the future, there will be more big data–based tools and services that bridge the divide between traditional media and digital media. Keep in mind that as TV becomes digital, we can use new technologies to help traditional TV and broadcast become more nimble and targeted. Take Bluefin Labs, which leverages insights from Twitter and Facebook to help advertisers know how well traditional broadcast ads perform in real time. This enables media buyers to update what and where they buy content, especially around marquee events that generate a lot of social media activity, like the Super Bowl, but also in more everyday programming. Using these kinds of tools, advertisers can tell right away if their ads work well on ESPN

SportsCenter or Lifetime. The Right Audience recently purchased by TiVo, enables advertisers to get as specific as an individual household and craft their ad approach accordingly. With big data analysis, they know whether a household watching SportsCenter contains Pepsi or Coke drinkers. This is done by using set-top-box data combined with real transaction–level data. For an even finer level of targeting, the data can be augmented with a client's CRM data. This can even be taken a step further, using the same targeting data and technology platforms that are required for display and digital media to help in target broadcasting. It's about the digital technology helping to get more value out of the traditional media, demonstrating an increasingly symbiotic relationship between the old and the new.

Convergence Catalysts

- Customer centricity needs to apply to media planning just as it does to other touchpoints. Where are your customers living? How do they want to be spoken to? What kind of voice are you giving them? All are questions to be asked as you think about how to allocate media budgets.
- Test and learn. Even TV advertisers can do this, as the Chipotle case shows. Use less costly digital channels to tell you what creative approaches are working and what aren't and then use this feedback to inform your traditional media buying.
- Long-term planning in the media business has been dominated by the upfronts. Like Steve Cannon, think about how forward-thinking media planning can be part and parcel of a long-term customer relationship. And don't allow your competitors to entrench themselves in new media because you don't see the short-term return on investment. Apply digital technologies that bridge traditional and digital media and interactions for better buying. In real time.

- Reserve some media budget for new channels. There is a tendency to spend as much up front as possible so as not to lose the budget. Resist this and hold back some budget to spend with new channels that arise in between your major planning sessions.
- Get out of the campaign mind-set and become an always-on publisher. The model here is to become more like a media company. It's as simple as using any number of off-the-shelf publishing tools in order to constantly engage with your customers.

Ubiquitous Computing

When, in spring 2012, Google released its concept video for a new project that would embed a computer in a pair of eyeglasses, you would be forgiven if you were a doubter. The prospect of a pair of glasses that doubled as a display for messages and performed searches and took photographs was not only too good to be true, it sounded like something plucked out of a mid-century science fiction novel. The announcement about Project Glass sparked a firestorm. Some users were excited by the augmented-reality technology. Some thought Google was once again touting technology that wasn't anywhere near shipping. And some thought it was an out-and-out fake.

The topic of wearable computers, like the entire category of ubiquitous computing (ubicomp), is subject to more overselling and disappointment than perhaps any other tech topic. Although most of us would love to live in a world where all of the nagging details of life could be managed by devices, we are far from being there, although it's been discussed, debated, and lusted after for decades. Progress has, for the most part, been painfully slow. Instead of flying to work with jetpacks every day, we fume over not being able to get a picture from a smartphone to be displayed on a TV screen. As such, it's easy to dismiss the concept as some far-off dream of science fiction fans. In truth, however, today we find ourselves on the brink of rapid innovation that is turning that dream into reality—and it may just be Google Glass that pushes us over.

In the months that followed the release of the concept video, it became clearer and clearer that Google was on to something. By the summer, Google cofounder Sergey Brin was showing off the glasses at Google's I/O show, telling the audience that a small group of early adopter types would be shipping the glasses in 2013. To whet their appetites, he hinted at the power of the glasses with a clever stunt—a live Google+ hangout featuring a quartet of parachutists who jumped out of a blimp above San Francisco and landed on the building where the Google I/O was taking place. Each of the parachutists wore Project Glass glasses that broadcast what they saw, as did stunt bicyclists and climbers who rappelled down the side of the building and joined the fun. Surprising even Brin, the stunt worked, a boon for extreme sports types looking for a hands-free way to record their extremeness. Other uses were discussed as well, including one that may resonate with more potential users than jumping out of a blimp: taking baby pictures. With a pair of glasses from Google, you no longer have to spoil any sort of intimate experience by rummaging around for a camera. "The baby looks into mom's eyes—they connect. While doing that, she can capture this moment without any distractions," said Isabelle Olsson, the Project Glass lead designer.

The glasses, light like normal sunglasses, have a side touch panel and a button to take photos and videos. The screen, which acts as sort of heads-up display, is transparent and off to the side so it's not obtrusive. Early reports from people who have played with the device suggest that wearing Google Glasses isn't tantamount to dipping your head in your e-mail. Rather, you can easily ignore messages when they come in.

As the months wore on, it became clear that reviewers were starting to fall in love with the device. *Time* put Google Glasses on its list of the best inventions of 2012, calling it "the device that will make augmented reality part of our daily lives."

Wrote Nick Bilton, in the *New York Times,* "I had a brief opportunity to try the glasses, and the experience was as mesmerizing as when I saw the iPhone for the first time."

This statement is crucial. If the iPhone, that nexus of design and computing power, was the first device to really showcase that potential of mobile technology, then Google's Project Glass could be poised to do the same for ubicomp. For decades, computing was all about staring at a monitor, typing on a keyboard, and moving a mouse. Then, around the middle of the last decade, it became about staring at your cell phone and then the tablet. In the future, computing will be less about having devices that mediate the act of computing. Rather, everything will have a computer in it.

"When technology gets out of the way, we are liberated from it," wrote Bilton. "Wearable computing will free us from peering at life through a 4-inch screen. We will no longer have to constantly look at our devices, but instead, these wearable devices will look back at us."

In this chapter, we examine the rise of ubicomp and what it means for business. Of all the topics we examine in this book, ubicomp is probably the most forward-looking. But it is also likely to cause big changes throughout your organization. Failure to understand what it means for your company's products, marketing, and customers could be disastrous in the long run, akin to not seeing the mobile revolution before it was here. Although stuff like Google Glass may seem far off, it isn't.

It may even be available by the time you pick up this book. The time is right, as John Seely Brown said to *Tech News Daily* in late 2010. Seely Brown is cochair at the Center for the Edge, and a former Xerox PARC researcher who helped coin the phrase *ubiquitous computing*. So he knows how much hype has surrounded the term.

"Prototypes are easy to make, but you have to wait for the magic moment, the special confluence when these things can hum without being a pain in the ass. And we're there now. We have a magic moment, a synergy, between the cloud, between how we build batteries, between how we use screens. All these different inventions are aligned now in a way that makes this a pretty exciting time."

FIGURE 7.1 Google's Project Glass Making Technology Part of Every Moment

Google's Project Glass is making technology available at the sound of our voice or movement of our head, not just enabling every moment of our life to be smarter, but also enabling us to capture and save every moment in our life.

What Is Ubiquitous Computing?

Back in 1995, one of Razorfish's cofounders said, "Everything that can be digital will be," offering a mantra for a new and growing digital marketing agency. Even back then this wasn't exactly a new idea. In fact, those exact words had been uttered a few years before by Barry Landa, an Israeli entrepreneur and founder of Indigo, which in 1993 unveiled the world's first digital color printing press, effectively bringing the printing industry that Gutenberg had invented 500 years before into the digital age. Indigo's new press, called the E-Print 1000, allowed for just-in-time and on-demand printing as well as customization and personalization. So when he predicted the digitization of everything, he added, "Printing will be no exception." (Having sold Indigo to Hewlett-Packard in 2002, Landa is now figuring out how nanotechnology can improve printing.)

It's fitting that this sentiment of uberdigitization originated with printing since so much digitization as we've known it has been about doing away with paper. Books, newspapers, and magazines have all been made nonessential by the rise of the Internet and devices that have converted reading from an analog process to a digital one. Music and movies followed, turning the consumption of media into a wholly digital experience for anyone who wants it that way. We don't have to tell you what the implications for the business world have been. But that was just the first wave.

In coming years, technology will digitize any and every touchpoint. Right now, the only computer that most of us carry around with us is our mobile phone. Before long, this short list could expand to clothes, accessories, and sports equipment, creating a computing wardrobe that turns our vital signs, weight, activity levels, and whereabouts into usable data. Meanwhile, our homes and offices will be increasingly tricked out with devices that are part of the Internet of things, a vast network in which previously dumb objects are embedded with sensors that allow them to communicate with other objects and, most important, with us.

The next 10 years will open unprecedented opportunities for the integration of tiny, inexpensive electronics into every corner of our lives. But we don't have to wait to see it. Let's look at few ways that ubiquitous computing is already reality.

The Home, Connected

Right now your home is as homes have been throughout history, a passive shelter that you live in. In the future, your home will be intelligent. It will listen to you and talk to you. It will know your patterns, your lifestyle, and your schedule. The devices that inhabit it will all be connected, ensuring safety, comfort, and convenience. You will receive alerts if something is amiss. The heating system will kick on when you're headed home from work. Over the next couple of years, we'll see more and more devices become digital, and then two to five years out we'll begin to enjoy seamless integration of all these devices, with an adoption rate of 50 percent.

Already we're seeing innovation here that should give you a taste of what's ahead.

The electronics giant Philips recently debuted Hue, an LED lightbulb studded with a tiny microprocessor that allows users to control brightness levels and colors in an ultragranular way through mobile apps. Then there's Twine, a puck-sized object loaded with sensors that helps users to monitor their home environment. Twine, with Wi-Fi, temperature and orientation sensors, and connectors for even more sensors, also boasts a Web app that's intuitive and requires no programming ability for setup. Users set up triggers to tell them if something isn't right. For instance, Twine could send you an e-mail if the basement floods, or a tweet if you've forgotten to close the garage door. Twine will start you out with a bunch of rules. For instance, when the moisture sensor gets wet, then text "The basement is flooding!" Next, it allows you to create your own rules that are shareable with the community of users. And Twine's most deluxe package sells for only $175.

The Nest Learning Thermostat allows you to control your heating and cooling system through its elegantly designed wall device—that's

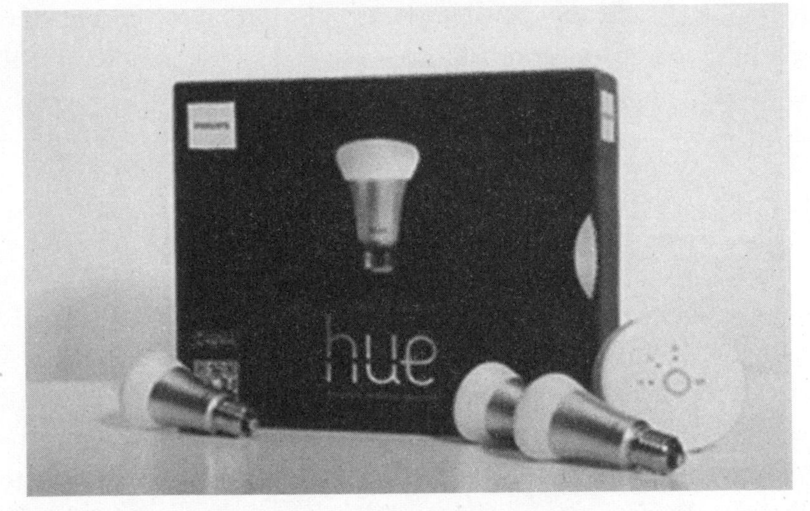

FIGURE 7.2 Phillips Hue Enabling Ubiquitous Computing

Phillips has rolled out a Wi-Fi–enabled smartbulb, taking us one step closer to the truly connected smart home.

the boring way—or it can be controlled remotely through a smartphone that accesses a digital profile that reveals insightful information about energy use that's shareable over social media (Figure 7.3). There's feedback between the device and the vendor, allowing the collection and analysis of massive amounts of usage data. Last fall, Nest, developed by former Apple executive Tony Fadell, rolled out its second version, which was slimmed and connected to more heating-and-cooling systems than the original. Nest's algorithms were also improved: Now motion detection determines when no one is home and tells the heating or air-conditioning to shut down. In the past this took 2 hours, but with the new version it takes just 30 minutes thanks to the ability to track patterns that show when no one is home. The company has said the thermostat now works with about 95 percent of systems installed in the United States.

The Self, Quantified

There's a growing group of consumers using technology to track their behavior in every facet of life: how much they sleep, what they eat, how much they work out, how much money they spend, and just about any other activity that can be turned into data. The growth of ubiquitous computing will only grow the ranks of the quantified self community.

> There's a growing group of consumers using technology to track their behavior in every facet of life.

A trend toward miniaturization will lead to a whole range of smart components that will be considered disposable. The low-cost factor is especially interesting for wearables, the integration of electronics into fabrics that opens up new dimensions for creativity. This is the sort of thing we'd wear every day that tracks what's going on in our lives and provides rich information about our surroundings without having to pull out our mobile phones. Nike has continued the digital integration initiated with Nike+ years ago, launching new

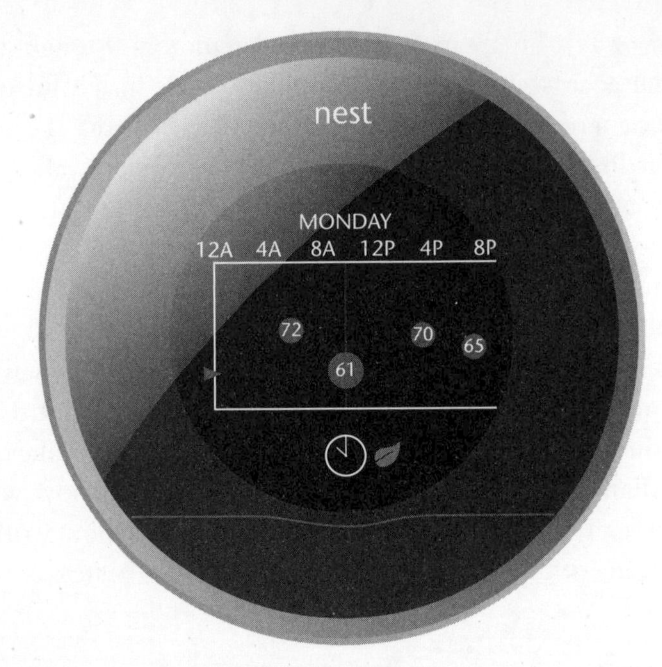

FIGURE 7.3 Nest Smart Thermostat

The Nest, on its second version in 2012, has an Internet-connected smart thermostat and uses your usage patterns with weather and proximity sensors to finally find the perfect temperature for your home, while smartly saving energy along the way.

extensions including Nike+ Basketball and Nike+ FuelBand. And Recon Instruments has built a tiny module that projects data about your day on the slopes right onto your goggles. Recon has partnered with Oakley to integrate the unit into its Airwave goggles so that skiers can see how fast they're traveling and have access to maps. They can check the temperature, control playlists, find out where their friends are, and see incoming calls and messages projected into their field of vision. All of this is displayed in the lower right-hand corner of the goggles so that it doesn't distract from the snow. To the eye, it looks as if it were displayed on a 14-inch screen 5 feet away. Users can respond to texts and calls with stock messages, such as, "Call you later."

GlowCaps are Wi-Fi–enabled replacement caps for prescription medicine bottles that help with compliance, a big issue in health care because patients are often less than reliable when it comes to taking their medication. GlowCaps, which essentially put a computer atop most standard prescription bottles, are meant to fix this. They use light and sound to signal when it's time to take your medicine and then they sense when a bottle has been opened. They issue reminders for when it's time to take a pill, and send updates to family members, doctors, and pharmacies, improving compliance with treatment plans. GlowCaps were even featured in a Museum of Modern Art exhibit about design in 2011.

Supermechanical, creator of Twine, has been working on other projects, such as Proverbial Wallets, a response to the virtualization of money. These are wallets that regardless of how much cash is in them—which, let's face it, has nothing to do with how much money we actually have—respond to your financial situation. So such a wallet might buzz in your pocket as transactions are occurring. Another wallet will become more difficult to open as you move toward your monthly budget limits.

Just looking at this list of innovations should tell you that there are a lot of players in the growing field of ubiquitous computing, from *Fortune 500* enterprises to 20-person startups to lone hobbyists. It's safe to say that this innovation will not necessarily be owned by multinational companies who have access to cheap labor around the world. Although the playing field for software innovators has long been rather level, the same isn't the case for people who actually want to make things. You might build your prototypes out of your garage in California, but you definitely won't be able to find a cost-effective way of getting stuff made in Palo Alto.

"Until recently, the ability to manufacture was reserved for those who owned factories. What's happened over the last five years is that we've brought the Web's democratizing power to manufacturing. Today, you can manufacture with the push of a button."

This is Chris Anderson talking to *Time* magazine (October 1, 2012[1]) about the rise of three-dimensional printers, which have been referred to as desktop factories that democratize the manufacturing process. Once prohibitively expensive, these devices have in recent years have gotten cheaper. Until recently, they were a six-figure purchase. In 2011, 3D Systems released a basic model called The Cube for $1,299. They work this way: You select a design of whatever you need to make and send it to the printer. After you choose from the available materials, perhaps rubber or a Lego-like plastic material, the printer begins making passes over the drawing, extruding the material and building the design layer by layer.

The list of objects created on these printers is growing: a wrist case that turns an iPod nano into a watch, any number of tools, shoes, jewelry, and chess sets—you name it. Jay Leno, a classic car enthusiast, has used his printer to create discontinued parts, while the Department of Defense has made aerospace parts. Architects use them to design models, and medical researchers even made a jaw that was implanted in a patient. These creations aren't going to put the global manufacturing base out of business any time soon, but they are game changing. Three-dimensional printers take rapid prototyping beyond something that's talked about on PowerPoint slides into reality. Quickly bringing an idea for a physical product to life, even if in a relatively flimsy fashion, can't help but speed up innovation cycles.

Chris Anderson is himself an interesting player in the world of ubiquitous computing. Until the fall of 2012, he was editor-in-chief at *Wired,* the monthly magazine about technology and innovation. From that perch, he wrote presciently about topics such as the long tail, freemium pricing strategies, and the growth of apps. The news that Anderson was leaving the much-coveted job to devote himself full-time to the drone manufacturing company he'd established was a huge validation of the maker movement. Anderson now oversees

[1]http://business.time.com/2012/10/01/how-the-maker-movement-plans-to-transform-the-u-s-economy/#ixzz2DMvkz4ZO

a company called 3D Robotics, a 40-person company with locations in the Bay Area, San Diego, and Tijuana, where the manufacturing happens.

In recent years, Anderson has been one of the biggest evangelists for the maker community. His grandfather invented a lawn sprinkler and won a patent in 1943, but it still took him seven years to bring it to market. Decades later, Anderson tried to make his own sprinkler capable of remote control via an app. It took a few months and $5,000. For Anderson, this is evidence of how all the digital innovation of recent years can be piped into the physical world.

"The past 10 years have been about discovering new ways to work together and offer services on the Web," he wrote in *The Guardian*. "The next 10 years will, I believe, be about applying those lessons to the real world. It means that the future doesn't just belong to Internet businesses founded on virtual principles but to ones that are firmly rooted in the physical world."

But not all those firms will be old-line manufacturers. The do-it-yourself (DIY) hardware-hacking maker movement is a subculture that drives the digitalization of physical goods and environments. Access to low-cost electronics and open hardware platforms (microcontrollers) such as Arduino and devices like three-dimensional printers enables these creative minds to innovate rapidly and bring ideas to life—making them akin to Silicon Valley's garage startups from the 1980s. Soon three-dimensional printers will be sold like the personal paper printers of today. By inserting electronics into previously "dumb" appliances, a whole world opens up for autonomous or connected prototypes that are shared online, presented at the Maker Faire (the Woodstock of DIY), or funded for mass production on Kickstarter.

The tension latent in ubiquitous computing can be seen in the tale of two watches. Last year, Sony hit the market with its SmartWatch, which allows Bluetooth communication between the watch and an Android phone. That means that smartphone functions such as messages, calendar, and e-mail will be brought right to your wrist. But there was much more excitement around a competitor product that was not only slower to market but slightly more expensive. The Pebble e-watch grabbed headlines when it became the largest Kickstarter project ever, raising more than $10 million from 68,000 backers. Its inventor, Eric Migicovsky, came up with the idea in Y Combinator, the well-known business incubator program, but was unable to raise funds for it from the usual venture capital sources. After putting it on Kickstarter last April, the initial fund-raising goal of $100,000 was reached in just 2 hours. Within six days it broke the Kickstarter funding record. As we write, the Sony watch is getting lukewarm reviews, whereas the Pebble, which hasn't even shipped, is sold out.

In summary, the open world of three-dimensional printers + microcontrollers creates a massive innovation opportunity similar to the way that the Web browser + HTML enabled a whole new digital economy. Three-dimensional printing technologies coupled with open innovation-sharing platforms such as Thingiverse enable the digitization of all things physical. As soon as someone creates the three-dimensional blueprint of an object and shares it digitally, others can do the same. Similarly, the Arduino movement is coupled with code-sharing sites such as GitHub and others, enabling the digital logic for creating new objects. For example, Chris Anderson's autonomous drone logic was made available to others throughout the world to build their own autonomous pilot drones, and more importantly, improve on that design.

How Business Can Respond

We tell you these stories like the one about Pebble not to scare but to inspire. For those of you in established businesses, ubiquitous computing is both a disruptor and an enabler. As with many of the technologies and trends we explore in this book, it's all about how and whether you use it. Innovation has been democratized—that's an immutable fact. You can take advantage of that by importing it into your enterprise or making the right partnership. Or you can risk disintermediation or worse.

As we've tried to make clear, you don't have to be a startup to thrive in a ubicomp world. Our more forward-thinking brands are already figuring out how to inject some ubicomp thinking into their products, services, marketing, and processes.

A great example of how ubicomp can be put to work for a brand comes from Mercedes, which is working to bring together customer and vehicle data. Its Customer Connect platform, expected in the latter half of 2013, will combine usage data—like how and when the car is driven—with vehicle data—the state of its components. Then, in the words of Steve Cannon, Mercedes-Benz USA, the company will "serve it up in a smart user interface" involving the driver's smartphone. Networking its cars will not only give Mercedes a huge amount of data about how products are actually being used, but it will also give customers the ability to get remote diagnostics. It's a platform that could be a huge differentiator for Mercedes in the luxury space of the market.

The task ahead of other organizations is to figure out where its ubicomp opportunities reside. The answer, naturally, depends on the business you're in. To help you get there, following are some practical tips for thinking about how ubicomp can be injected into your organization.

- **Digitize your physical environments.** There's already a lot of this going on and we discuss this at great length in our commerce chapter. One example is augmented reality—layering digital content on top of the physical world when viewed through a camera-enabled digital device such as a smartphone. Another is Apple's use of iPads in its retail stores to replace static signage. The devices not only provide detailed, interactive product information but also let the shopper page a salesperson for assistance. You can take this further by equipping salespeople with iPads or Square-enabled iPods, essentially giving them all the product and customer information they need to make their sales right at their fingertips.

  These advances represent the beginning of environments themselves becoming digitally connected, creating much deeper integration than existing location-based services. Businesses of all kinds can benefit from this universal connectivity, and it will quickly become a customer expectation. Now is the time to take a closer look and reveal hidden potential within businesses. Identify potential touchpoints for consumers and build communication channels around them to empower platforms that generate valuable insights and facilitate a smoother experience.

A great example of the digitized environment is the AT&T flagship store in Chicago. In its 10,000-square-foot space there are 150 synchronized displays, including a 20-foot interactive wall, creating a wall-to-wall interactive experience. This store does a great job of showing how technology enhances the customer experience across the AT&T products and services available to their customers.

- **Reinvent experience design.** When the iPhone was launched, touch was a relative novelty. Within a few short years, it has become the expectation. Consumers tend to move quicker than most businesses and they will be enjoying the benefits of ubicomp before your company knows what's going on. A company's commitment to staying on top of increasingly pervasive technologies and placing smart bets will be key to its survival. How much is too much? When is a little not enough? Big questions loom for those who shape user experiences. The increased focus on simplicity requires the removal of features, often making the consumer feel like they have lost control. We'll see devices that try to be to smart but fail, leaving the customer annoyed. It will take careful experience design considerations to strike a balance between simplicity and control.

Remember three important changes wrought by ubiquitous computing:

1. **Devices will interact with you, not the other way around.** Right now, our devices are typically passive. We activate them to perform a certain task. In the future, devices will initiate

communication with the user, sending messages and alerts and information based on habits, decisions, and preferences.

2. **Devices will sense and react to the user's environment.** Thanks to location-based services, devices will know where you are and deliver content and solutions accordingly.
3. **Devices will connect with each other seamlessly.** Gadgets will automatically communicate with each other, transferring information and optimizing, delivering a seamless and integrated experience.
4. **The experience-design ethos that follows from these factors is the natural user interface**, that is, the idea that the relationship between the human and machine should be as frictionless as possible. At its best, ubicomp will simplify, not complicate, by helping to make technology seamless. Abstraction and complexity in traditional user input, such as the keyboard and mouse, will give way to intuitive experiences that are less feature-driven, require less attention and feel more natural to use. In the future, we'll be touching, tapping, and speaking our way to better tech interactions. Vision-based systems such as motion sensing or face recognition can make interactions smoother and more intuitive. As we've seen with Microsoft's Kinect and other systems, interfaces can leverage gestural interactions that range from subtle facial expressions to full body movements, with an increasing awareness of context. Face and body analytics can be gathered entirely behind the scenes and generate insights about age, gender, and other demographic traits—so that automatic targeting methods can further simplify the experience.

- *Think omnichannel.* Consumers are already expecting seamless experiences that move from desktop to mobile and back again. They expect digital-style personalization, instant gratification, utility, and communication from physical environments. Ubicomp will fuel this further. Although most brands are just now wrapping their heads around how to deploy across mobile and desktop Web environments, it's already time to think about deploying to other digital channels, like connected TVs and physical environments. Context and personalization are probably the most important keys to unlocking truly magical experiences, but you have to remember to understand the tension between privacy and personalization.

Start an episode of *30 Rock* upstairs, then pause it, go downstairs, and pick it up from the very point where you left off. This isn't yet as easy as it ought to be, and there are both technical and business-model challenges impeding progress. But tech like Apple's AirPlay begins to show the possibilities. This device allows users to wirelessly transport video from an iOS device to a big-screen TV via Apple TV. Pushing content from handsets to other screens, projectors, and speakers is another step toward frictionless content sharing.

This challenge has increasingly been on advertisers' minds. Microsoft recently unveiled Polymorphic ads, in which creative elements are assembled to fit various formats from the PC and Windows 8 apps to the Xbox and mobile devices. The idea is to have a creative idea that flows consistently across multiple devices, formats, and sizes. It's also a way for us to make any environment our own—personalizing the space with a high level of control and customization. This is especially important for environments in which we rely on media—including cars, airplanes, hotels, and conference rooms. Razorfish's own 5D platform is another example of fluid content, enabling consumers to effortlessly engage with retail brands across multiple devices. The 5D platform, unveiled at the 2012 NRF Convention and Expo, connects digital devices such as kiosks, large-screen displays, tablets, and personal smartphones to better attract consumers into the store, drive product engagement, and arm store associates with more contextualized digital tools. It allows content to be moved from a store-owned touchscreen to a customer's mobile device and vice versa, while facilitating commerce.

Digital out-of-home ads can suddenly become approachable in a way that allows passersby to instantly grab some piece of information being advertised, or easily take part in a campaign. By lowering access barriers and making it easier to take away and share brand and product information, retailers can regain some control over the digital in-store experience, and nudge the social sharing habits of their customers. NFC enables physical "tap gestures" for instant connectivity, taking greater advantage of devices in close proximity. In some markets, especially outside the United States, contactless payment has already taught people to "tap to pay." Soon, "tap to connect" or "tap to share" will allow consumers to conveniently consume digital information and services advertised in physical proximity, a problem that quick response (QR) codes and printed URLs were intended to solve.

- *Evolve product development.* Ubicomp isn't just impacting how you market your products. It needs to be built into the very product itself. As everything becomes connected, Web services like e-commerce, software updates, and social connectivity are suddenly accessible, even to analog products. Hardware can unlock additional features on demand through one-time purchase or subscription models. These features were previously only available to websites and traditional software. Platforms and APIs need to be built as a foundation for enabling communication infrastructures between vendors, devices, and end users.

The context for which you're developing products is changing rapidly. You're no longer developing products for a living room or a kitchen but for something bigger, an Internet of things. So it's not just a question of how will my product be used by a consumer, but how will it play with the other objects he or she owns? How can it be integrated with mobile apps? How will it resonate in social media? What kind of data implications are there?

Convergence Catalysts

- Digitize your physical environments. Begin with commerce, where mobile point-of-sale displays are already growing more and more popular with retailers and there's a natural fit. Develop an omnichannel content and API strategy, making sure that your content translates well for different devices and contexts. The API strategy enables your brand to stay connected and relevant with all appropriate aspects of your customers' lives. If you manufacturer apparel, you can better understand your customers' closets, an appliance manufacturer can know more about appliance quality, an auto manufacturer can know more about driving patterns, and so on.
- We suggest that product-driven companies go out and get their hands dirty with Arduino and other inexpensive electronics microcontrollers in order to identify new opportunities for smarter product lines that will drive innovation for years to come.
- Back some Kickstarter projects. In some circles, Kickstarter gets a bad rap as a place where filmmakers, artists, and musicians go to grovel for pocket change. The reality is that there's a ton of innovation there around the bridge between the digital and the physical. Join up and you can see it as it unfolds. There's no replacement for backing a project. Ponying up gets you on the inside so that you can see how the project came to be, how it's coming together, and how it's getting marketed.
- Buy your company a three-dimensional printer for your office. Take advantage of the steep declines in price and begin rapid prototyping or maybe even rapid manufacturing.
- Make it a point to go to Maker Faire, the two-day geekouts that now happen all over the world. At these celebrations of the DIY mind-set, you'll find plenty of innovation and inspiration. As with Kickstarter, increasingly Maker Faire will spawn your future talent, partners, and competitors.

The Road Map

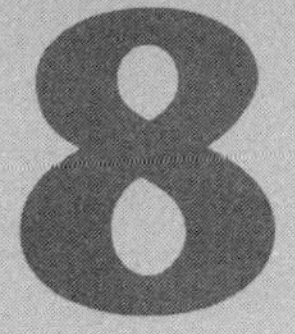

8 Creating a Religion around Convergence

Until now, we've been laying out the ideas central to convergence. We've explained what this coming together of media, technology, and creativity is and what it means to your organization and the business world at large. We've showed you some companies that are dealing with this dramatic shift well and some who aren't.

Now, in the book's final chapters we're going to draw you a road map. This map will take you from where you are now, most likely an organization built for a predigital age, to one that's better engineered for the rapid innovation and disruption cycles of the twenty-first century. The road map will address both broad strategic issues and down-and-dirty tactics. We'll teach you how to recast your organizational ethos, and we'll tell you how to get executives involved in the change even if they don't want to be part of it.

We'll start off by talking about how you can develop a vision of change, telling you how to think about this, who needs to be involved, and how the vision needs to be articulated. We'll follow by looking at how your organization and its processes need to be made over. It's not enough to just tell you to blow up your silos. We'll tell you exactly how to do it. Finally, we'll end with a discussion of Agile methodology, which we believe is key to establishing a customer-centric organization built for our time.

The Convergence Mantra

It all begins with a story.

To effect real change, you need a narrative that you can tell to all interested parties both upstream and downstream, to both your bosses and your subordinates, to the people who will sign off on it and those who will execute on it. This story, if crafted and told well, will become your organization's mantra and act as a constant reminder of the long-term vision and the mind-set it takes to achieve convergence.

Why do we call it a mantra? We're of course being metaphorical here. In Eastern religions, especially Hinduism or Buddhism, the mantra clears the way for transformation in activities like yoga or meditation. It's a tool that calms and focuses—and those virtues should prick up the ears of any executive in today's harried, chaotic business environment. The mantra is also easily remembered and repeatable and sharable. And you will return to it again and again amid the din of transformation.

A great company doing this well is Zappos. Under the inspirational leadership of Tony Hsieh, Zappos has created an amazing convergence-based culture. If you remember back in Chapter 1 we talked about how the highest priority catalyst for convergence is to put your consumer at the center of it all. Which is exactly what Tony has evangelized at Zappos and the mantra around which he has organized his team. Lucky for us he has talked about how he and the team did in his book, *Delivering Happiness*.

Zappos has always taken an unconventional approach to customer service. Rather than have a scripted customer service team or a hard to find phone number, Zappos has broken the mold. A quick Internet search will show dozens of amazing customer service stories, everything from sending flowers to customers on their birthdays to overnighting—for free shoes to a best man who forgot his shoes for his buddy's wedding. All of this happens because Tony has the quiet leadership to create happy employees who result in happy customers.[1]

---

[1]http://articles.businessinsider.com/2012-01-09/news/30606433_1_customer-service-zappos-center-services

The happy by-product of this approach for Zappos is that their customers are on average more loyal and more profitable and just as importantly more vocal. They are sharing their positive experiences broadly across the Web, driving traffic back to Zappos and increasing search rankings at the same time. In fact, Tony has said his approach is to take dollars that would have traditionally been spend on paid advertising and marketing and apply them to the customer experience.[2]

So how has Zappos helped drive the mantra throughout their organization? Well, it's through a grassroots approach that empowers every employee. New employees go through over seven weeks of training. And to make sure they are committed to the company goals, they are offered $2,000 to quit a week into the training. Supposedly only 2 to 3 percent take Tony up on it, but the offer is more about setting the tone of the culture.[3]

Find Your Visionary

Remember how we said that your mantra has to flow both upstream and down? Well, you need a leader who can make that happen, who gets how marketing and technology can come together, and who can communicate the benefits of that convergence. That leader needs to understand that the real value of data is that data tell us what the customers want and, more important, what they are doing. And, of course, the customer doesn't care if they are interacting with the booking engine or the loyalty engine, so neither should your organization. Reengineering for convergence requires massive investments in time, money, and energy.

> Reengineering for convergence requires massive investments in time, money, and energy.

[2]http://www.deliveringhappiness.com/about-us/frequently-asked-questions-answered-by-tony/

[3]http://www.businessweek.com/stories/2008-09-16/why-zappos-offers-new-hires-2-000-to-quitbusinessweek-business-news-stock-market-and-financial-advice

Long-existing structures need to be pulled up like stubborn tree roots. Egos need to be massaged in some cases and given a swift kick in the butt in others. Spending on talent and technology needs to happen. And convincing others within the organization that all that incremental spending is worth it is no mean feat.

Figuring out who's going to fill this role is not easy. Sometimes it helps to have fresh eyes from another industry. But insiders can get the job done, too. Steve Cannon, our Mercedes client, has been with the automaker for the majority of his career, rising from executive assistant to CEO. As we mentioned earlier, his leadership has enabled Mercedes to more effectively organize around convergence.

Turn Outward and Workshop, Workshop, Workshop

Your mantra should be informed by your competitive environment, but not limited by it. You need to look outside your organization and your competitive set. Too many enterprises are inwardly focused, not just on their own struggles, but on those of their immediate rivals. In being laser-focused on their top three or five market-share nemeses, they're closed off to the outside world. And that's a big mistake.

We live in a time of great innovation that's all unfolding in the public eye. Genuine, honest-to-gosh businesses are being built in a matter of months. Others are being destroyed just as fast. You need to take in the landscape. Where are the destructions coming from? The inspirations. It's no longer enough for Pepsi to simply pay attention to Coke. They both have to look out for the new player that will upend everyone. Remember what happened to the music industry. The record labels were too concerned with each other to see the digital downloading revolution coming. The signs were there, but the industry wasn't paying attention.

Turning outward isn't about playing defense. It's also about seeing and understanding what's working for innovative companies and adapting those lessons for your organization. Ford CMO Jim Farley has talked about how he looked to the video game industry for inspiration and observed how prelaunch strategies for big games could do the same for his model launches. To some degree, that's heresy to the auto business, where conventional wisdom holds that you shouldn't promote new products lest consumers ignore ones in the market. With the Fiesta, he brought in social media influencers well before launch—as happens with many video game marketing programs, where journalists routinely write about early versions to gin up the hype.

The lesson: Take an outward-looking perspective and epiphany after epiphany will follow. Workshopping will help this along.

Razorfish's strategy practice is workshop-driven. We typically do a minimum of three workshops over the course of an engagement. First, there's the opportunity assessment, in which we paint the landscape and size the pools of opportunity. Then comes strategy development, where we craft shared bets and decide where to place bets. Then there's prioritization. For this, we get a broader cross-functional group in the room to see to which story everyone is going to gravitate.

Build a Big Boat

There's a famous scene in the movie *Jaws*, where Chief Brody finally gets a glimpse of the enormous predator. Stunned by its size, he mutters to his fellow shark hunters, "You're gonna need a bigger boat." You're going to need a nice-sized vessel as well, although for different reasons. The challenge of organizing for convergence won't bite you in half—probably—but it will require lots of cooperation from lots of different parties. After all, a converged organization is by definition a collaborative one in which silos are porous, not rigid. It is only logical that this organization will be attained through a similar ethos of collaboration and openness.

Doing a lot of strategizing prior to this could be a big waste of time. No one wants to be clued into a change in strategy after that strategy has already been developed. We see this often and it often puts convergence efforts back to square one.

First things first: Get your grassroots efforts going. You can't be the only one speaking the language of convergence. You need to find who else is likeminded in your department or function. Who are the other agitators? Who else believes in a collaborative converged model?

Then begin to bring in all the parties who need to be part of the convergence conversation. Think of it as three different tiers, each of which should cross-functional from the get-go.

First, there's the core team that will have day-to-day responsibilities in pushing things forward. Functions that need to be represented are marketing and IT, of course, and digital if your organization has one. The makeup of your company will also help to decide if you need additional representatives. If you're a retailer, you'll want representatives from diverse merchant categories. If you've got a large portfolio of consumer goods, you'll want the biggest brands present.

Then there's a tier of participants who are actively consulted with but aren't part of the day to day. Corporate communications or public relations might be included in this because so much of convergence is about social interactions. Another is sales or, in certain organizations, dealers or franchisees, agents, or brokers—the folks who are on the hook for the revenue. There might be secondary brands who want to have a say but don't need to be in every meeting.

The final tier is a group of stakeholders who are involved at the beginning and again when plans are more fully baked. Included here are legal and compliance representatives and an executive steering team that might be composed of the CIO, CMO, and CFO. The CEO will be involved from time to time and, if the change is fundamental enough, so will the board of directors.

If this sounds like there are a lot of cooks in the kitchen, that's because there are, necessarily. Because of that reality, it does help to have an external party who can keep things moving. But this can also be someone internal who can act as an arbiter or a facilitator.

A couple of key points in blocking and tackling: Watch out for necessary people who aren't taking part in the process. You've heard the expression about there being no atheists in the foxholes. Well, there can be no conscientious objectors in convergence. Make it impossible for them not to participate. Keep them updated and create an e-mail trail of your efforts. See if you can get the CEO to force them to play along.

Another point: Don't forget finance and legal. Here's one of the biggest mistakes we see repeatedly. You have great technology and vision. Finance comes along and asks about how much it is going to cost. And no one has any idea. The remedy is simple. Bake in finance from the beginning to establish not just the business case but something that's going to pass muster with the CFO.

That said, there are some caveats. The finance representative has to be interested in the business and not just a bean counter with the dream of being senior controller someday. He or she needs to have an operational mind-set, and cannot be someone who just manages finance for a particular brand or product line. We're talking about someone with access, and someone who is fluent in both revenue and costs and how the organization capitalizes them.

Legal also has to be included and taken seriously. This is especially the case when social media is playing a big role or when you're in a heavily regulated industry, such as pharmaceuticals or alcohol. It's especially important to have IT and legal together on the question of how regulations manifest themselves in the technology infrastructure.

Write Your Road Map

Over the past 5 or 10 years, everyone, not just IT, began using road maps. We'd contend, with apologies to John Wanamaker, that the road map is the new advertising. Half of it is wrong; you just don't want half. Here are some thoughts on how to get it right.

- Clients want three-year road maps. And, in a way, that's good. You want to be looking down the road. But the reality is that more than 12 months down the road, we have no idea what the external world is going to look like—what marketing tools are going to be available or how consumer behavior has changed. Perhaps the time frame is shorter. "The three-month road map is about the best horizon you can be thinking about coherently," Box founder Aaron Levie has said.

  But this isn't an argument against having a long view. Instead, we're urging you to take that long view with a grain of salt and know that part of it is going to be wrong. And know that it's a mistake to treat every year of that road map equally. You really want to be stronger on the first year, essentially knowing your release plan over the first 12 months. At Razorfish, we develop a 12-month road map with our clients, but cycle and review that road map every month. It really becomes a living business strategy document so that we can respond to the ever-changing marketing and technology worlds.
- Many road maps are concerned with technical dependencies to the exclusion of other important considerations, such as financial concerns. The financial story of the road map is very important and if you're not building it in you're not doing it right. When do you break even? When do you see positive return on investment? When do you need to recalibrate?
- Inherited road maps are a tricky business. As a change agent, you need to be aware of what's in them and who owns them. Who had a seat at the table in informing the road map? Road maps can be touchy. Often, they're not well understood even though they were developed at great cost by a consulting firm that has long since departed.
- Finally, you need to be flexible about road maps. When you're on month three and already falling behind, the road

map becomes an albatross nobody wants to talk about. It can even become a barrier to getting stuff done. Agile practices, which we'll discuss later, are the antidote to some problems with road maps. But all in all road maps need to be living, breathing documents, and there needs to be a well-defined process for having a conversation about where you are and what needs to change. When new technologies are introduced or a sudden change in the economy happens, your road map must adjust. For example, overnight Ford's owner priorities went from helping owners deal with the gas price hikes to understanding owners' need to focus on keeping their cars longer, and the company started looking for extended warranties from the credit crisis. Android overtook iOS as the top smartphone platform in just months, not three years.

When Telling Your Story, Think Right Brain and Left Brain

The failure of traditional approaches to strategy is that you end up with a thick binder of charts, graphs, and big blocks of text that will probably end up gathering dust. You need that binder, but there are other tactics that will better rally the organization.

We've found that visualizing strategy through videos or perhaps an interactive room that depicts a retail environment helps. Clients are sometimes reluctant to go down this road, but we find increasingly that they want it. It's something tangible and rich and easy to deploy. And it helps your convergence evangelists by allowing them to tell the story by just pushing play. We've even had one of our videos reenacted on stage at a client's 20,000-person sales conference.

Alongside that, you need a financial model. This is a business case for the changes you're describing. Otherwise, you're just talking.

Visualization + financial is what makes change possible.

9 How to Change Your Organizational Structure

So you've got your convergence mantra, you've prioritized your projects, and you've figured out how to tell your story. Now what?

You may immediately be struck by the rather unpleasant feeling that you're unable to make the changes you know you need to make. Perhaps you don't have the right personnel in place. Or maybe it's a matter of job descriptions: No one is tasked to perform the work you need to get done. If your company was born in the pre-Internet era, it's very likely that your organizational structure is ill-suited to develop the projects on your lists. Maybe there're past failings telling you that this kind of convergence experience won't work within the setup you've got. Or it's the simple realization that you're not equipped to make the changes you need to make.

So how do you change this?

For many enterprises, the dis-integration of marketing and technology is a root cause of much dysfunction. It's the culprit behind missed deadlines and the reason for why projects stall and fail. It explains why the experiences that brands created don't live up to expectations. Throughout this book, we've talked about breaking down the silos, and although we're serious about the sentiment, we're also being slightly hyperbolic for effect when we use terms like *blowing up* silos. Of course, we're not asking you to strip your organization free of structure. That would be encouraging a form of business suicide. Organizational charts don't go away, not even in an enterprise optimized for convergence. In those enterprises, the structures and silos are more rational and better oriented to understand and respond to the customer journey. They breed accountability and cooperation and they're focused on providing the customer with what they want and need.

In this chapter, we're going to offer some remedies for organizational atrophy.

The Rise of the Chief Digital Officer

It would be impractical for us to suggest that all your problems will be solved by having stand-alone digital operations overseen by C-level executives with a direct report to the CEO. But it is worth talking about this setup, if only to get you thinking about a trend that's sure to unfold over the next few years—the rise of the chief digital officer (CDO).

Nor are we arguing for tossing out the roles of the CIO and CTO. We are arguing that marketing and technology functions need to work better when it comes to creating customer experiences. For an increasing number of enterprises, this cooperation is achieved through a digital operation, overseen by a CDO. These days, the C-level title is perhaps being adopted most quickly by governmental and academic institutions. Most corporations have been slower to adopt the nomenclature, with the exception being agencies and media companies that, faced with the very clear-cut challenge of porting and reinventing legacy analog businesses for a digital world, have been leading the charge.

Generally, the role is to live at the technological intersection of the enterprise and consumer and oversee a digital operation that's separate from the legacy organization. What is needed is someone who can act as a tech-savvy guru and manager comfortable with a lot of dotted-line reports.

Although it is no small matter to add a new C-level role, we are seeing more and more of them. Gartner predicts that by 2015, 25 percent of organizations will have added the role to their C-suite. With some early indications that having a CDO can result in real innovation, this number could get even higher.

In March 2012, Starbucks created the CDO role, reporting directly to CEO Howard Schultz and responsible for core digital businesses across Web, mobile, social media, card, loyalty, e-commerce, and Wi-Fi. Adam Brotman will also lead the company's emerging in-store digital and entertainment teams. At the time of this announcement, Starbucks was pretty far from clueless when it came to digital. Starbucks was already doing a heady business in mobile payments and it had a strong social media presence. But Brotman's presence took innovation to the next level. It followed quickly with big bang news: a $25 million investment in Square along with an agreement that would have the payments provider handle all its debit and credit card transactions. In November, this rolled out to 7,000 stores. Before you knew it, Starbucks was the subject of headlines that called it a tech company.

"Right now, there's a lot of excitement among combined digital teams for the opportunity to innovate and build upon a foundation that started with My Starbucks Idea and exploded through social media," Brotman told *VentureBeat* in June 2012. "The true opportunity is in how we combine all these things. One group . . . one direction."

That's a great way of thinking of the role of the CDO. It's someone who can take a company's scattered digital businesses and assets and coordinate them, while ensuring that they don't get bogged down in the organizational in-fighting that can go on in legacy functions. The CDO will also be crucial as the trend of ubicomp takes hold. (See Chapter Seven.) He or she will have to work across all organizational areas, from operations to digital commerce to physical commerce, touching everything from the integration of new mobile payments systems to leading the way on developing a product portfolio integrated into the Internet of things.

Bottom-Up Solutions

Your organization may not have the resources or even the desire for a CDO and you may be able to live without a standalone digital organization. What's important is that "one direction" that Brotman mentioned, and different companies achieve it in different ways.

Even if your organization can't change at the C-level—or can't change fast enough—there are many bottom-up strategies that can be deployed rapidly to get you underway to more harmonious organizations. A few of these are described in the following.

Create Cross-Functional Project Teams

This is a way to get marketing and technology collaboration happening fast. Get all the relevant players on a team with a clear shelf life and deliverables. Maybe it evolves to become a permanent team structure focused on digital experiences; maybe it won't. The key is to get people working together where they haven't before.

Create New Roles within Both the Marketing and IT Functions

The approach here depends on where you sit within the organization. Within the marketing department, you can hire a chief marketing technologist, a new title whose responsibilities might range from making display advertising more effective to coordinating data programs. The marketing department can hire tech-conscious product managers or creative technologists who bring expertise in the experience layer, the tech that supports digital experiences but not the core enterprise IT infrastructure. Finally, a marketing department can hire data scientists, not just experts in running regression models but also in how data warehouses are set up and how to architect them. IT, historically all about security, stability, and redundancy, can shake things up by hiring people who specialize in that digital experience layer.

Moreover, there's an opportunity here to help each other become better shoppers. We all need to stipulate that tech is changing rapidly and nobody has a handle on it. Marketers often don't know how to buy tech. They don't know how vendors and pricing works. IT doesn't get the speed and customer-centricity that's essential to marketing. If marketing is hiring a chief marketing technology officer to help bring more automation to bear, IT is hiring someone who's an expert in marketing platform solution suites. Both sides win. Ideally, you encourage marketing and IT to start trusting each other and driving toward the same goals. Hackathons where IT and marketing work through the night together help teams on the ground better understand each other's challenges, while enabling great innovations to bubble up within organizations. Ideas can come from anywhere but need cross-disciplinary input.

Employ Internal Account or Relationship Management

In this schema, a person in marketing has a corresponding person in IT who can be sought out when there are problems. Internal points of contact are created. Think of it like a cross-functional buddy system. The digital lead for each brand has a go-to person in the IT organization. This also begins to change the talent mix because it means marketing has to hire a tech-savvy digital marketer and IT has to hire someone good with digital platforms and not just an expert in Outlook.

Here are a few specific examples of how clients are tackling marketing/tech collaboration issues. At Mercedes-Benz USA (MB), CEO Steve Cannon installed a 14-person customer experience group culled from existing teams to help, in his words, "carve through silos." Mercedes-Benz is obsessing over the customer experience, trying to ensure that it's consistent from the company website to the mobile experience to the dealer floor. To create this team, he pulled from marketing, from the group that works with dealers, from after-sales, and from other silos as well. The idea is to get a holistic understanding of how Mercedes-Benz is serving its customers.

"Unless someone is monitoring the whole, all of a sudden you get a clunky thing," Cannon said.

That team is there to optimize the system. How? One example: When Cannon found out that all the departments were standing up different surveys, he blew that up. In total, MB surveyed 4.3 million people. All these well-intentioned silos and some departments couldn't describe what they were doing with the results. "Let's combine those surveys and drive down cost," he told us. "I'd rather have 500,000 that I can use as intelligence." MB created a Digital Center of Excellence last April to facilitate best practice sharing.

"If something's working well," said Kevin Biondi, "we make sure it gets channeled throughout the organization." Biondi has also used the center to improve Staples' digital analytics effort, helping improve marketing effectiveness.

"We can get better, cleaner insights on how marketing is working, which translates into shifting investment into the most effective marketing vehicles."

A *Fortune 50* enterprise we work with that has struggled with serving customers through its website as efficiently as its rivals chose a different path. Rather than blow up its entire organization, the company moved the 500 or so people from marketing and IT teams responsible for a single product to a different location and put technology media and marketing side by side. The change in location communicated that their jobs had changed. The goal was that they better understand the customer experience and improve. Thus far, it's resulted in simplified interactions with potential customers, reducing the amount of friction. And innovation is happening on a daily basis to provide their consumers with new tools and products.

Each of the approaches in the examples is distinct and right for the organization, but there is a common thread that runs through them. One is customer-centricity, which needs to inform everything that a modern marketing organization does. Digital is a lever for this.

Establish a Collaborative Culture

"You're not going to be able to do it alone." That's Frans Johansson's advice to CIOs as they are asked to take IT out of the role of mere tech support and into a more strategic place that touches every function of the modern organization. But we'd all do well to listen to those words.

In Chapter One, we mentioned that Johansson's 2006 book, *The Medici Effect,* has been an inspiration to us as we think about where business is going. Late last year, we talked to Johansson about how the ideas might become practice. He consults with a large swath of the *Fortune 500*, so he's had plenty of insight into how companies fall down as their culture becomes more collaborative and their teams more heterogeneous.

One of the key things to remember is that heterogeneous or cross-functional teams don't progress at the same rate as homogeneous teams do. Homogeneous teams progress in a linear fashion and then reach a low peak. For cross-functional teams, especially newly constructed ones, there is often an S-curve—a slower rate of progress early on as the team comes together and people from different functions get used to working with each other followed by an explosion. But it's important to remember that the cross-functional leader is not running a touch-feely perpetual brainstorm. Real collaboration can yield long ideation periods that at some point need to be clamped down so that the team can execute.

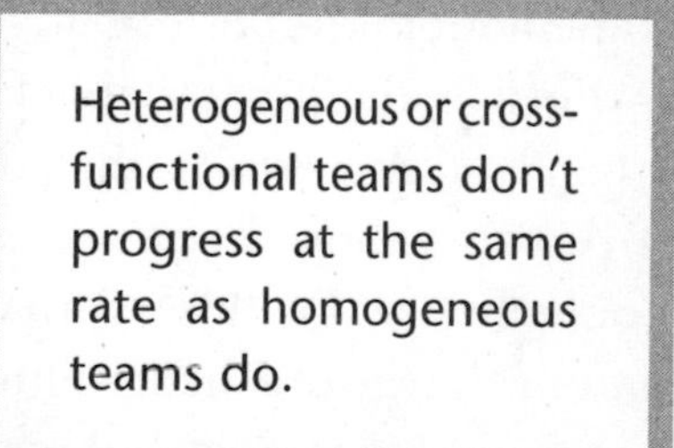

As a way of illustrating collaboration in action, Johansson talked to us about Dice, the video game publisher known for the *Battlefield* series. After one of the company's animators read *The Medici Effect,* Dice began implementing some of its principles. In the original setup, animators and programmers sat apart from each other and they communicated about specifications and so forth through e-mail or paper. Dice changed this and within two weeks they started seeing results. The award-winning and very popular games

Mirror's Edge and *Battlefield 3* were built under a setup that had pods of people working in tandem around the company. Now animators can communicate directly with programmers and vice versa.

Once you've got the structure, then you need goals. When it comes to goal setting, Frans advises that you set a goal immediately, but be ready to challenge and reexamine it. "The more time sitting around talking about it, the more time that's wasted," he said.

If all the different functions have different ways of defining success, should you just create new objectives? Yes, says Johansson, advocating that companies call a "time-out" for incentives. The leadership needs to let the team ignore the specific goals and deadlines on current projects and create a separate pot of money for the project in question. Doing this short-circuits any arguments over which department is footing the bill for which cost.

But that doesn't mean that the new project is the recipient of some bottomless pot of budget. "The rule we give is that you have to do it without extra money and within your current job. Only when an idea merits it, then does it break away."

As we wrapped up, we asked Johansson what kind of proof points he has for this approach. He surprised us by telling us that he once created a hedge fund that managed a portfolio based on companies' success at embracing diversity and collaboration. "It did really, really well," he said, but he got out of it because he "didn't want to be in hedge funds anymore."

Johansson believes that people do things because of emotion, not because of data. When it comes to management, there are firms that hire only Harvard Business School graduates. But on what basis is this a good idea? To them, it should be just obvious, but these companies didn't make this analysis based on a spreadsheet or ROI. They just thought it was the best course of action. "People rarely do something because they've been shown the data for it," he said. "It happens, but it's not the overwhelming impetus."

He paused and added a point to ponder for anyone doubting the power of collaboration: "I've never heard anyone ask for the ROI of a homogeneous team," he said. "No one ever asks me for that."

How to Change Your Processes

No amount of big talk about convergence will matter unless your organization has the right processes to guide it on a day-to-day basis. Unfortunately, few do. Most plan and budget for the long term in a way that doesn't respect today's lightning-quick innovation cycles. They fail to take advantage of a marketing ecosystem that allows for real-time optimization and constant reiteration. In this chapter, we'll describe the specific steps you need to take to get the right processes in place to embrace convergence.

1. Change Measurement and Establish Objectives

You're about to make a lot of big changes and cause a lot of disruption in your organization, likely causing some queasiness among those used to doing things the old way. There is a need to be able to demonstrate that these changes are having a concrete impact on the business. What you need is a shared measurement framework. Or if you already have one, you might need to optimize it or tidy it up.

A call for measurement may have you worrying about a huge new outlay. This step doesn't necessarily entail huge incremental spending. Many companies who aren't measuring properly are already spending many millions of dollars on Oracle and Omniture. It's just that the investment isn't well deployed. Fixing it is often a case of doing better with what you have, remediating your current systems, and getting more out of it. It might be switching on your always-on research tools—listening platforms and the like. Execution is crucial.

One of the important things here is making sure that the measurement framework is shared. Too often we'll hear that a measurement system is already in place. When we ask to take a look, we'll get an answer along the lines of the following: "It's complicated." "There's one guy who has access and he's never here." We're exaggerating, but you get the picture. Measurement needs to be relatively open access, transparent, and something close to real time. We're advocating getting multiple functions to rally around a shared set of objectives and a shared method of measuring process—that's a big change and it has to be tracked cleanly and carefully. You also don't want to have to conduct a science experiment every time you want to see how things are working. Thus, you're getting your systems to feed a dashboard that tracks these five metrics. Then you have to get the team to check in regularly, or at least pay attention to the readouts they're receiving.

Measurement needs to be relatively open access, transparent, and something close to real time.

You want your people to have incentives around shared objectives, not objectives in silos. They need to be shared goals so it's clear we're all in this together. And targets need to be fair. It's not fair when digital is held to a greater return on investment accountability than traditionally, or physical store commerce is expected to get higher margins than digital commerce.

2. Change Planning

Too many companies are stuck in an annual planning-only mode, another remnant of the slow-changing analog media world that required lengthy periods of planning and creative development with media budgets and campaign ideas locked down long in advance.

In those days, it was all about the big idea. Now it's about a big idea expressed in many ways that is created in collaboration with consumers and molded in an ever-changing technology world. The articulation of your idea is two-way (at least) and changing month to month, if not day to day.

Moreover, the future of marketing will be marked by a shift of money from working media into what we'll broadly define as marketing operations. In the past, marketing ops were largely limited to the maintenance of an internal marketing team and hiring and firing agencies that produced the creative work. In a converged world, it will be about those activities, but also about investing in people and systems to ensure that the marketing spending is optimized. In the old days, people were accountable for spending the dollars, not how well they were spent.

Now you need to think of planning this way:

- Annual planning
- Quarterly executive reviews and recalibrations
- Monthly checkups
- Weekly stand-up meetings for the marketing team
- Daily scrums and real-time changes
- Product backlog prioritization sessions

This is just a general model. Every organization will attack planning differently. But the important point is true for any organization: You need to be planning across a range of different timescales. Each timescale is crucial and will enable your organization to become nimble and frequently revisit to see what's working and what's not.

For IT and marketing to work together, alignment of plans is key. Put the functions' respective road maps together, and align them as well as the budget. Everyone is grappling with change. Grapple with it together, rather than separately.

3. Change Budgeting

You need to change your budgeting process in a way that mirrors the overhaul to your planning processes. This isn't just a question of shifting money around in media silos. It's not just turning TV ad buys into banner campaigns. There's a fundamentally different type of spending here. Ultimately, you'll be taking money away from media and putting it into operations. In other words, it will be less about Super Bowl ads and more about software. This is tricky, given that marketing organizations are still incentivized around billions of dollars of ad spending.

Besides funding people and systems, you need a slush fund to react to stuff. You need money in reserve for programs you don't know you want to do yet. Here you'll want to start small. After all, in a world of measured media planning, you'd be crazy to have any money in reserve because you couldn't get it into the market until the last minute. You'd be stuck holding a bag of money and you'd get in trouble for not spending it. The key here is to begin with 90–10, then go to 80–20 and so on.

If you do change your media mix in a big way, you need to be doubly sure you've invested in the systems capable of proving that as you migrate to a different mix, the world didn't end. If you can't prove it, a conservative organization will conclude that anything bad that happened in the business cycle is a result of you not spending the money in traditional media.

4. Think Like a Software Company

Thinking like a software company means remapping your organization around product management. This is exactly how many of our clients have approached it. For most organizations the title *product manager* is a new addition to marketing and technology teams. In fact, it's more befitting a tech company than a traditional enterprise. As we've mentioned a few times now, you need to imagine your company as a software publisher, increasingly under pressure to frequently update, test, and learn, and to respond to real-time consumer feedback.

Adopting a product manager approach means that there will be accountability for each step along the consumer journey. Much like there is someone at Facebook who owns the News Feed, there is someone at your organization who owns the tablet experience or the website. In convergence, change is going to be perpetual. With a product manager setup, it is someone's job is to manage that change both as representative of the silo but also as a broader organization. There is a process to developing talent to think like a product manager.

As one of our clients describes it, product managers have to understand the customer and constantly prioritize and re-prioritize against what's best for the customer. It's such an important skill that organizations like the Scrumalliance, a professional organization created to share the Scrum Software Development processes, have created a course to help train people on product management. Across Razorfish, we continually see it as the top challenge when executing with an Agile and iterative methodology.

Finally, once you have the right people in place, they need to be empowered. If people looking at data aren't empowered to make changes, you're dead in the water. If you have to go through an IT organization's unwieldy process, it doesn't matter how good the data is because you can't react quickly.

5. Change Incentives/Compensation

One of the clearest messages you have to send is this: Convergence isn't some sort of hobby to be done during downtime. The way to ensure that it happens is to change the way that team members are compensated by building in a system of goals and incentives that reflect the changing nature of what it is they're doing.

It's worth noting that this is a sensitive process, not only because you're tweaking the stuff of people's livelihoods. Compensation changes touch parts of the broader organization that you might not be used to dealing with in a meaningful way—most notably, the human resources department. Much like IT, human resources is slow to change. It's a function not known for innovation; it just keeps the paychecks coming. As a result, the function has often been treated like a group of clerks, even though it should have a large role in culture setting. Nevertheless, human resources has to be made a strategic partner in all this.

Personal Goals

The shared measurement framework that everyone is working off of has to be translated into all team members' personal goals so there's a clear sense of individual and team missions, and with this the basis for changing performance reviews. At least in the early days, you'll most likely be adding goals, not wiping out the old ones. So, marketers might already be tasked with affecting traditional marketing metrics, such as raising brand awareness, and techies will have their corresponding metrics, such as maintaining uptime. Those don't necessarily change or go away—at least at first. Instead, you'll be adding goals that relate to the work of cross-functional teams and getting your team members to weight them as equally important if not more important. Of course, this needs to be done in such a way that the new goals don't contradict the old ones.

It's important to note that this isn't just about picking on predigital goals. It's just as important that a marketer whose goals are exclusively digital—such as reducing cost per click—ends up thinking about convergence goals, such as raising customer satisfaction and so forth. It's about getting away from legacy goals that are solely based on marketing channels, whether digital or analog, and thinking about team-based outcomes.

Pay

The goal here is to shift incentive compensation away from legacy functional or business unit goals to cross-functional goals. We write this knowing that this is a big idea that requires fundamental organizational change. But the reality is that for any employees whose bonus rests on old thinking and goals, they will not invest themselves in the new goals.

The overarching problem is that in most cases, at least some portions of bonuses are pegged to stuff that's going on at a functional or department level in a way that encourages behavior that props up silos. Another problem lies in the fact that bonuses hinge too often on things the people can't control. You have to bring it down a level. In general, you want to weight incentive compensation to stuff that people can actually control.

Remember, though, that pay is not the only thing that matters. It might not even be the most important if you subscribe to the rather large amount of research suggesting that focusing too much on pay can actually demotivate people. The organization becomes focused entirely on quantitative goals and monetary compensation and neglects extrinsic motivators. These are the big questions: What do you want out of life? What gets people out of bed in the morning? Extrinsic motivation is about helping your team members answer those questions in a way that also moves the organization forward. Some ideas follow:

- Cultivate innovative "hot teams" and give them the trappings they need to be set apart from the rest of the organization. The classic model here is Apple's old Macintosh development team that moved across the street and famously hoisted its pirate flag.
- Give people a break from the legacy role, with a temporary leadership role or a rotational assignment in another geography, or find some way to satisfy their entrepreneurial urge.
- Organize an exchange program with other functions. Spend a year in IT, if you're a marketing person.

Review Process

We begin with the proposal that you ditch the once-a-year review focus in favor of more frequent feedback sessions. Although there still needs to be a top-down, quantitative assessment of whether a team and its members hit the goals that were set, relying on numbers alone may seem like you're operating a forced march. There also needs to be a peer component that looks not at key performance indicators but at how the team performed as a team. That means team members evaluate each other. This, to be clear, isn't about money, but rather about developing an understanding of just how well the team is functioning as a team and benchmarking how well the team comes together over time.

11 Achieving Convergence through Agile Methodology

Throughout Chapters 8 through 10, we've hammered home a few central themes:

- Organizations need to be more cross-functional and collaborative.
- They need to work faster.
- They need to be more responsive and flexible.
- They need to be more accountable.
- They need to try, fail, learn, and succeed.

By now you might be nodding in agreement even as you realize you have no actual clue how to bring this sort of change to your business. The answer, we believe, is Agile. You've surely heard of it and maybe even flirted with implementing it. Maybe you've even tried large-scale deployment or a pilot and watched it crash and burn. We've referred to Agile a few times, and now we want to explore at length how you can use it in your organization, regardless of the industry your organization is in.

Within Agile, cross-functionality is ensured because Agile teams can be cross-functional in nature. That correctly built Agile team, comprised of user experience, technology, and a business owner, can be tweaked within enterprise marketing and IT environments to include the relevant roles and functions. But regardless of a team's makeup or the exact flavor of the Agile being used, adhering to the methodology's main principles will help your organization become more customer-centered.

Historically, enterprise IT backlog has moved too far away from the customer, often aligning with business needs that have nothing to do with the customer experience. Agile IT ensures that won't happen. An Agile marketing organization is always on and responsive and is not driven by campaigns locked in a year ahead of time. Marketing managers become product managers driving a backlog of customer-focused needs while negotiating how to address technology debt and requirements. The Agile organization plans on timescales from the daily to the annual and is always testing and learning, accountable to finance, and data-driven.

Remember, regardless of your place in the organization, customer-centricity is your north star. Agile can get you there.

What is Agile?

Agile is a software development methodology inspired by lean manufacturing and product development principles. Having read that you may find yourself wanting to skip ahead, especially if you're not in the software business.

That would be a mistake.

If you think that because you work in soft drinks or banking or cookies, you can't learn anything from software development, you're dead wrong. You only need to look at your phone to understand the future of marketing. If you've got an iPhone, the App Store icon will likely have a little red numerical indicator on it telling you just how many app updates are waiting for you. It's a constant and somewhat nagging reminder of how software is a living thing, continually being adapted to new ecosystem requirements, to user behavior and the moves of competitors.

Increasingly, this will become true of all marketing outputs, not only apps. You need to release code all day, every day, like a startup would. You need to constantly rejigger your ad campaigns based on consumer reaction. You can't do this with traditional planning and project management. But with Agile, you can achieve the speed and flexibility you need to thrive in an iterative world.

There are four central benefits of Agile: the ability to release early and generate new ideas quickly, the ability to release more frequently, the ability for user testing to influence subsequent design cycles, and the ability to change the vision of the product as it comes to life. Together, these benefits can give you the power to build what emerges as the most valuable features rather than what was concepted before design and development began. When a product can be used, tested, refactored, and conformed to an evolving vision, then the likelihood of building what users need and want increases substantially.

There are four central benefits of Agile: the ability to release early and generate new ideas quickly, the ability to release more frequently, the ability for user testing to influence subsequent design cycles, and the ability to change the vision of the product as it comes to life.

A simple truth of software development is that it often fails. As reported in its 2012 Chaos Report, the Standish Group found that between 2002 and 2010, only 37 percent of software projects were successful, where success is defined as delivering the desired functionality on time and on budget. Twenty-one percent of those projects failed, and 42 percent were deemed challenged. Those are pretty bad numbers.

The picture does, however, change meaningfully when you apply a different lens and consider not merely whether the projects worked but what product management methodology was being applied. For our purposes, we'll consider two different methodologies: waterfall and Agile.

Waterfall is linear and sequential and is defined by a series of self-contained phases. First come requirement specification and design, then coding and testing, followed by installation and maintenance. Each phase must be 100 percent complete before moving on to the next. The waterfall model's heritage is in traditional (non-lean) construction and manufacturing, inherently noniterative activities because after-the-fact changes are so costly. The waterfall process defined project management in hardware development and software as well, at least until the 1990s, when Agile started popping up.

In 1995, developers Ken Schwaber and Jeff Sutherland presented a paper that described scrum methodology, a set of guidelines and processes for managing complex projects often used in Agile development. Hirotaka Takeuchi and Ikujiro Nonaka wrote in the Harvard Business Review in 1986: "Under the rugby approach, the product development process emerges from the constant interaction of a handpicked, multidisciplinary team whose members work together from start to finish. Rather than moving in defined, highly structured stages, the process is borne out of the team members' interplay."

In 2001, the Agile Manifesto was published after 17 developers gathered at a ski resort in Utah to chat about how a slow, documentation-driven software development process could be made over. They came up with an 11-point plan, the first of which sums everything up: "Our highest priority is to satisfy the customer through early and continuous delivery of valuable software."

Since then, Agile has grown quickly, with all kinds of different flavors sprouting, and more and more companies have adopted it. Agile coach Joe Little maintains a running spreadsheet and lists more than 200 companies that use Agile, including American Express, Bank of America, Nokia, Xerox, and too many media and tech companies to name. Electronic Arts is one well-known practitioner. The game designer used scrum and kanban to develop the physics engine that breathes life into many of its games.

Why has Agile become popular? Because it works. In cases where the waterfall process was being used, the success rate was only 14 percent, according to Standish. In cases in which Agile was applied, success was three times more likely: 42 percent. And the failure rate declined, precipitously too, from 29 percent under waterfall to 9 percent under Agile. That's a decade's worth of data to show that Agile is a more efficient way to go about software development.

Why does it work? Agile and iterative Web development were built to solve business issues by focusing on enabling change and learning from real-world feedback.

Commonly used waterfall processes assumed that the business would stop changes when development entered the design process. That's why commonly used processes fail—they require business and product owners to lock in decisions before they start using the technology. If innovation stops after the concept and design phase, this approach locks your business and users away from your product during the building phase. Success requires an iterative ongoing process, taking a hard look at the concept and product as designed and continuously innovating. Business and marketing priorities change as users get their hands on your digital products, and incorporating those changes back into the product builds trust with your consumers and creates opportunities for innovation.

It's often a difficult reality to swallow, but nothing speaks more loudly than real-world analytics. With studies from respected companies such as the Standish Group showing that 64 percent of designed functionality rarely or never gets used, it's easy to see that the big bang approach to building digital products and marketing experiences wastes a lot of time and money. Following an iterative approach enables our focus on the highest priority items in every release.

Agile's four simple principles, derived from the Agile Manifesto (http://agilemanifesto.org/), solve business needs. These principles are summarized in the following.

Individuals and Interactions over Processes and Tools

Focus on the ability to communicate and review work as opposed to getting document sign-offs. Traditional processes assume rigid change order processes and documentation. Agile focuses on constant communication over working software as opposed to low-business-value documentation. This is the real opportunity with Agile and convergence; Agile focused on individuals and collaboration as a way to successfully deliver on software-based experiences and applications.

Working Software over Comprehensive Documentation

Since communication is at the heart of Agile, comprehensive documentation isn't needed. Light documentation with constant communication will enable more business value and ability to change. The focus is on what is absolutely necessary as opposed to detailed documentation that is out of date before it's published.

Customer Collaboration over Contract Negotiation

This does require extensive customer involvement, but that's a much more useful focus than haggling over whether a feature was in the original statement of work. With Agile, the customer is prioritizing all potential features at the beginning of every sprint. Agile won't build all the features on the list and therein lies the value. Why build them all when a relative few are used?

Responding to Change over Following a Plan

By breaking up what traditionally would be a six- to nine-month detailed design and development process into one- to three-week sprints, the process allows for drastic changes in direction. A good example of this is a project we did for Ford Motor Co. At the beginning of the project, gas prices were at an all-time high, so one of the key features was highlighting fuel economy. Midway through the project, gas prices were on the decline and broader economic issues were impacting the nation, so the focus shifted to information like monthly payment and special financing offers. Using Agile, we were able to respond to that change without building a wasted set of features around high gas prices.

How We Use Agile

At Razorfish, we've used Agile processes for years for clients such as AT&T and Ford. It was crucial in our development of Bundle .com, the personal finance venture that helps consumers manage their finances by giving them unprecedented amounts of comparative spending data. The joint Bundle.com/Razorfish team worked out of a development lab in Razorfish's New York office to quickly develop a beta version in time for a January 2010 launch. The other unique piece of Razorfish Agile is that we have extended the process to support cross-disciplinary roles. Most traditional training programs on Agile never mention a creative director or an experience designer; our approach integrates them intrinsically so we can make sure we are driving true innovation.

Later that year, we formalized our Agile practice, and the following year, we rolled out its next iteration, an enhanced variation of Agile scrum development. The offering integrates teams from Razorfish's nine U.S. offices with the agency's near-shore locations in Argentina and Costa Rica. This provides the same cost advantages as offshore development but also delivers key advantages such as continual innovation, leaner delivery teams, and increased collaboration.

We saw two competitive advantages here. First, our teams are near-shore, meaning they are located in the same time zone as their U.S. counterparts, which allows for daily real-time meetings and updates. Second, Agile+ incorporates our creative and user experience teams throughout the process, which shortens time-to-market and fosters innovation.

By the time we'd announced the news, Razorfish had already leveraged Agile+ in more than two dozen projects for clients such as Choice Hotels and Mercedes-Benz USA, in various development capacities, including e-commerce, content management, and mobile implementations. After seeing it in action, Choice adopted the approach postproject to drive efficiency in its own development cycles. As part of the ongoing evolution of the practice, Agile+ has now been rolled out to all U.S. and near-shore Razorfish offices. Razorfish has also developed and deployed several Agile+ Scrum workshops that are used both internally and offered to clients.

The Razorfish Agile approach is a recommendation for incorporating the Agile methodology within a consulting-based project framework. It works because it aligns user experience, creative, and development. It allows for a period of project definition and contract negotiation, a visioning phase where the project strategy is defined, and finally, the iterations for designing and building the product. Figure 11.1 represents a sample schedule for these activities.

During the foundation sprint, while the core technology tasks are being performed (infrastructure code, environment setup, etc.), the design team is establishing the visual design language

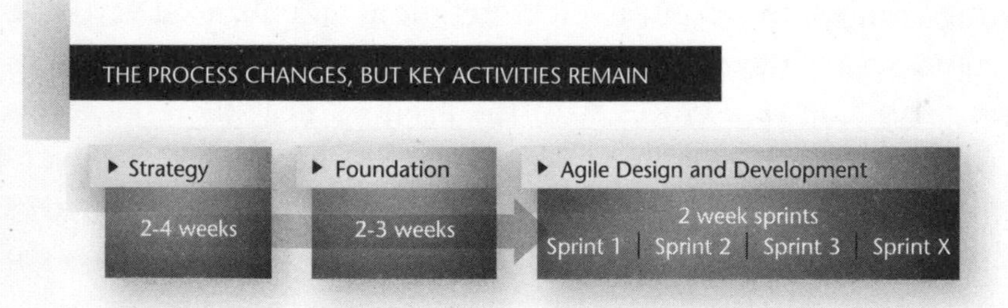

It remains critical to set the overall vision upfront, but convergence is about moving into iterative design and development as quickly as possible. Convergence success depends on continuous learning and testing, which is only possible through iterations.

FIGURE 11.1 An Iterative Approach

and sketching the wireframes that correspond to the highest prioritized user stories. This allows the design team to get the head start needed to ensure that the development team has the elements needed for subsequent sprints. Maintaining this pace allows design to lead development while development still impacts design.

Another Benefit of Agile Lies in How It Facilitates Communication

Although everyone would like to have the entire team in one room, it's not possible these days. One reason that teams often need to work from distributed locations is the increasing need to leverage the lower rates charged by developers in other parts of the world. Global delivery and offshore certainly have cost benefits, but there are other reasons why distributed teams are needed. Computer science graduation rates have slowly been decreasing over the last 10 years and needs have not been shrinking accordingly (see, for instance, "America's Tech Talent Crunch," by Dice, at http://marketing.dice.com/pdf/Dice_Tech TalentCrunch.pdf). That's only part of your team, with business, user experience, creative input, and delivery all likely to be in multiple locations.

Using a process that affords enough communication to ensure success is required. E-mail, instant messaging, video conferencing, conference calls, and collaboration tools all have a role in keeping in touch, but at their core, clear communication, in which all members of the team know what they need to do and everyone else knows what they are doing, is necessary.

Two core tenets of scrum that help tremendously in these areas are the sprint backlog and the daily stand-up. An updated sprint backlog, preferably hosted so a real-time version is available to all team members at all times, keeps the entire team up to date on what everyone else is working on. Not only does this help from a management perspective but it also helps the team know exactly who to contact to troubleshoot problems, offer assistance, or take over work if other issues or needs arise.

The daily stand-up, possibly the most borrowed component of scrum, gives the team the chance to know not only what everyone is currently working on but what was accomplished the previous day, what the members of the team have planned, and whether there is anything preventing them from completing their work. Ensure that requirements are clear, work is reviewed frequently, and issues are resolved quickly.

Hand-in-hand with communication is ensuring that rapidly changing requirements are understood by the team at all times. Waiting for documentation to be updated, or waiting for time with the stakeholders to communicate changes to everyone involved, often comes at the expense of development efficiency.

Sprint planning at the beginning of each sprint or iteration not only ensures that the team has the time to plan the work that will achieve the desired outcomes but also gives the team time with the product owner to clarify requirements and solve potential issues early.

Another risk associated with working with offshore resources is potentially not knowing the quality of the work until it is completed—when it's too late. Scrum not only divides the development cycle into small enough units to help mitigate this risk but also provides within its core processes a way to handle those situations upon review of functionality. If the acceptance criteria are not met, the issue is returned to the backlog to be addressed in the next sprint.

Successful project approaches maintain enough flexibility to change over time to leverage new findings and team strengths. This is especially true when working with offshore resources where the developers may be new to the organization or process. Scrum provides recurring reviews of not only the work but the process: when the approach isn't working, change it.

Sprint retrospectives allow the team to highlight what is working well and what needs improvement. These improvements, when they can be implemented, can have an enormous impact on the team's productivity. Changes can bring about a better way to accomplish something, but they can also significantly raise morale when team members know that feedback is valuable. The biggest value is our ability to actually learn and adapt our process. Iterative approaches teach estimates as estimates and enable project teams to increase their certainty of development times and give the product manager (the role formerly known as marketing manager) more trust in the ability to prioritize.

How to Get Started

Chances are, you're not going to become an Agile operation overnight, but there are things you can do in short order to begin the process:

- **Educate yourself.** By this point, there are hundreds of books on Agile, not to mention workshops, webinars, and other educational resources. Become a scrum master or a product manager through a scrumalliance.org course. Razorfish has a 3-hour cross-disciplinary workshop we use internally and with clients that can help introduce a full iteration in just a couple of hours with hands-on involvement.
- **Pilot a project.** Get an Agile team formed around a particular project with a clear desired outcome. Certain kinds of activities lend themselves better to Agile than others. They include Web and software development (of course), but also digital marketing activities, including display advertising and e-mail campaigns, and social media programs. Agile works there because these kind of marketing channels are all about testing and learning and iteration.
- **Don't get hung up on the particulars**. Agile is a process with well-established principles and practices. In your initial experiments you should hew as close as possible to these: Do your daily stand-up, visualize your project, and plan in terms of

sprints. At the same time, don't get hung up on the finer points. If you lose six months because you're going to send 200 people to a workshop, or you're arguing over whether your scrum master needs to be certified, or wondering whether you actually have to be standing up at the stand-up, then you're missing the point. Agile should be inspirational and aspirational, not a drag.

- **Get an outside partner.** For certain projects at Razorfish, we've essentially become surrogate Agile teams. We'll populate roles and work in Agile ways, in which the client is the stakeholder and we check in with them. It's a way to see the Agile process in action while reducing risk to your timeline.

Convergence Catalysts

Getting Religion around Convergence

- Write your story. This is a vision of organizational change as defined by competitive threats from rivals both known and unknown—your nearest peer in market share and those two guys in a garage looking to take out your business.
- Find your visionary. The executive who can communicate the vision both upstream and downstream.
- Turn outward and workshop. Don't limit your analysis to the category competitive set as it currently manifests. Look at disruptive threats on the horizon or try to steal from innovation in other industries.
- Build a big boat. Determining who needs to be part of your shift to convergence is crucial. To be cross-functional and cross-disciplinary you'll need to consult a host of functions that might seem ancillary now, from legal to finance to human resources. Find like minds in those departments and start to build them into the conversation as soon as possible.
- Develop your road map. A three-year road map won't hurt, but it is the first year that you need to focus on. It really becomes

a living business strategy document so that you can respond to the ever-changing marketing and technology worlds.

Changing Your Organization

- Hire a CDO. This won't be possible for every organization, but having a C-level executive who can aid with the technology tsunami will help.
- Create cross-functional project teams. Get everyone used to working together. Have clear objectives and deadlines.
- Create new roles with marketing and IT functions. Begin to blend the functions by injecting tech into marketing and marketing into tech. Consider a chief marketing technologist.
- Employ internal accounting or relationship management. This is a buddy system in which each key marketing staff has a corresponding go-to person is technology and vice versa.

Changing Your Processes

- Change measurement and evaluation objectives. From the beginning you need to ensure that you have a clear, working measurement system that connects to a dashboard and reflects progress on a set of shared goals.
- Change planning mentality and approaches. Planning needs to happen not just annually but across several timescales. Make sure marketing and IT are conscious of each other's plans.
- Change the budgeting approach. Get out of the mind-set where the entire budget has to be committed as far ahead as possible. Reserve 10 percent for spending on projects that are last-minute additions.
- Begin to think like a software company. Your inspiration in all of this is the Silicon Valley disruption that's fast-to-market, releasing often, testing, and learning.
- Change incentive and compensation systems. Make goals about the team, not just the individual. Consider both intrinsic and extrinsic motivators.

Adopt Agile Methodology

- Educate yourself. There's no shortage of information about Agile. Read a book or take part in a workshop to understand the philosophy, the application, and the vocabulary, of which there is no shortage.
- Pilot a project. Create a cross-disciplinary team, set your goals, and get going.
- Don't get scared off by the particulars. Do your daily stand-up, visualize your project, and plan in terms of sprints. But don't get hung up on the particulars. The project won't fall apart if you sit down during a stand-up.
- Hire an outside partner. Sometimes a third party will help you learn and implement Agile methodology faster than you could on your own. You may need help filling all the roles you need to have filled on the team.

Final Thoughts

So you've followed our road map to a tee. You've cleaned up your organization to eliminate needless, unproductive, and even harmful silos. You've scrapped all those old processes that were established in a pre-Internet marketing world. You've become more cross-disciplinary and cross-functional, bringing a greater range of voices to the table. And you've begun to implement Agile methodology. You're finished, right?

Wrong.

As you begin to adapt your organization for convergence, you'll quickly grasp the reality that this job is never really finished. It's a constant cycle of testing and learning, building and destroying. A central truth of convergence is that it is a constant, never-ending process, not unlike the forces of evolution that ensure our natural world is in a perpetual state of flux. In much the same way, media is rapidly changing. Old outlets decay, while new platforms pop up. But new ones don't remain new for long and they're quickly pushed aside in favor of the newest new thing. The same is true of technology, with ceaseless innovation in the cloud, in social media, and in big data, ensuring that we'll never get bored. This is so even when not mentioning the impending maker revolution, which will impact every object in our physical environment. Meanwhile, creatives have at their disposal a continually refreshed arsenal of new tools and techniques. It follows that brand experiences will need to be constantly refreshed.

Keeping up with all this might seem like a dizzying prospect, but it doesn't have to be. Winners in the twenty-first century won't be distinguished by how fast they master buzzwords or how many faddish new digital marketing campaigns they undertake. Those winners will be organizations whose main focus is on their consumer's journey and who possess a relentless desire to understand and improve that journey from beginning to end. This isn't merely about serving up new ads cloaked in the latest social fashion but about improving the consumer experience at all stages. Nor is it about having an A-to-Z understanding of every new technology that comes along. The trick is understanding the advantages and limits of those technologies and being open to experimenting with them. Rather than stay married to the old way of doing things, embrace change and think about how tech innovation can be put to work to benefit your customer. Approach technology the way a consumer would, without fear or favor and with a sense of wonder and curiosity. And always remember that if you follow your customer you can't go wrong.

Glossary

A/B testing A/B testing or split testing compares the effectiveness of two versions of a Web page, marketing e-mail, or the like, to discover which has better response rate or better sales conversion rate. A classic direct-mail tactic, this method has been recently adopted within the interactive space to test tactics such as banner ads, e-mails, landing pages, or even entire websites.

Adobe Adobe Systems Incorporated (/ə'doʊbiː/ ə-DOH-bee) (NASDAQ: ADBE) is an American multinational computer software company headquartered in San Jose, California. The company has historically focused on the creation of multimedia and creativity software products, with a more recent foray toward digital marketing solutions.

Agile management Agile management or Agile project management is an iterative method of determining requirements for engineering and IT development projects in a highly flexible and interactive manner, such as Agile software development. It requires empowered individuals from the relevant business, with supplier and customer input. There are also links to learn techniques, Kanban, and six sigma. Agile techniques are best used in small-scale projects or on elements of a wider program of work or on projects that are too complex for the customer to understand and specify before testing prototypes.

Agile Manifesto In February 2001, 17 software developers met at the Snowbird, Utah, skiresort to discuss lightweight development methods. They published the Manifesto for Agile Software

Development to define the approach now known as Agile software development. Some of the manifesto's authors formed the Agile Alliance, a nonprofit organization that promotes software development according to the manifesto's principles.

APIs An application programming interface (API) is a protocol intended to be used as an interface by software components to communicate with each other. An API may include specifications for routines, data structures, object classes, and variables. An API specification can take many forms, including an international standard such as POSIX, vendor documentation such as the Microsoft Windows API, and the libraries of a programming language, such as Standard Template Library in C++ or Java API.

App A mobile application (or mobile app) is a software application designed to run on smartphones, tablet computers, and other mobile devices. They are available through application distribution platforms, which are typically operated by the owner of the mobile operating system, such as the Apple App Store, Google Play, Windows Phone Store, and BlackBerry App World.

or

Application software, also known as an application or an app, is computer software designed to help the user to perform specific tasks. Examples include enterprise software, accounting software, office suites, graphics software, and media players. Many application programs deal principally with documents. Applications may be bundled with the computer and its system software, or may be published separately.

Amazon's Elastic MapReduce Amazon Elastic MapReduce (Amazon EMR) is a Web service that enables businesses, researchers, data analysts, and developers to easily and cost-effectively process vast amounts of data. It utilizes a hosted Hadoop framework running on the Web-scale infrastructure of Amazon Elastic Compute Cloud (Amazon EC2) and Amazon Simple Storage Service (Amazon S3).

Analytics Analytics is the discovery and communication of meaningful patterns in data. Especially valuable in areas rich with recorded information, analytics relies on the simultaneous application of statistics, computer programming, and operations research to quantify performance. Analytics often favors data visualization to communicate insight.

Arduino Arduino is an open-source, single-board microcontroller, descendant of the open-source Wiring platform, designed to make the process of using electronics in multidisciplinary projects more accessible. The hardware consists of a simple open hardware design for the Arduino board with an Atmel AVR processor and on-board input/output support. The software consists of a standard programming language compiler and the boot loader that runs on the board.

asset utilization The asset utilization ratio calculates the total revenue earned for every dollar of assets a company owns. For example, with an asset utilization ratio of 52 percent, a company earned $0.52 for each dollar of assets held by the company. Increasing asset utilization means that the company is being more efficient with each dollar of assets it has. This ratio is frequently used to compare a company's efficiency over time.

associative barriers The inability to connect different concepts across fields.

availability zones To make EC2 more fault tolerant, Amazon engineered availability zones that are designed to be insulated from failures in other availability zones. Availability zones do not share the same infrastructure. Applications running in more than one availability zone can achieve higher availability.

EC2 provides users with control over the geographical location of instances that allows for latency optimization and high levels of redundancy. For example, to minimize downtime, a user can set up server instances in multiple zones that are insulated from each other for most causes of failure such that one backs up the other.

High-availability database services, such as Amazon Relational Database Service, run on top of EC2 instances.

ATG Art Technology Group (ATG) was an independent Internet technology company specializing in eCommerce software and on-demand optimization applications until its acquisition on January 5, 2011. ATG continues to be based in Cambridge, Massachusetts and operates under its own name as a subsidiary of Oracle. ATG's solutions provide merchandising, marketing, content personalization, automated recommendations, and live-help services.

AWS Amazon Web Services (abbreviated AWS) is a collection of remote computing services (also called Web services) that together make up a cloud-computing platform, offered over the Internet by Amazon.com. The most central and well known of these services are Amazon EC2 and Amazon S3.

back-end Front-end and back-end, in addition to their obvious use in everyday English, are generalized terms that refer to the initial and the final stages of a process. The front-end is responsible for collecting input in various forms from the user and processing it to conform to a specification that the back-end can use. The front-end is an interface between the user and the back-end.

bid management systems Bid management is software used for the automatic controlling of bids in search engine marketing (SEM). With a bid management tool, any number of search terms (keywords) can be managed via various paid search providers (e.g., Google AdWords or Yahoo!). The system automatically transmits changes to bids to the relevant channels, such as Google AdWords, via API.

cloud computing Cloud computing is the use of computing resources (hardware and software) that are delivered as a service over a network (typically the Internet). The name comes from the use of a cloud-shaped symbol as an abstraction for the complex infrastructure it contains in system diagrams. Cloud computing entrusts remote services with a user's data, software, and computation.

The Cluetrain Manifesto *The Cluetrain Manifesto* is a set of 95 theses organized and put forward as a manifesto, or call to action, for all businesses operating within what is suggested to be a newly connected marketplace. The ideas put forward within the manifesto aim to examine the impact of the Internet on both markets (consumers) and organizations. In addition, as both consumers and organizations are able to utilize the Internet and intranets to establish a previously unavailable level of communication both within and between these two groups, the manifesto suggests that changes will be required from organizations as they respond to the new marketplace environment.

cluster A computer cluster consists of a set of loosely connected computers that work together so that in many respects they can be viewed as a single system.

content management system A content management system (CMS) is a computer program that allows publishing, editing, and modifying content as well as maintenance from a central interface. Such systems provide procedures to manage workflow in a collaborative environment. These procedures can be manual steps or an automated cascade.

contextual advertising Contextual advertising is a form of targeted advertising for advertisements appearing on websites or other media, such as content displayed in mobile browsers. The advertisements themselves are selected and served by automated systems based on the content displayed to the user.

CFO The chief financial officer (CFO) or chief financial and operating officer (CFOO) is a corporate officer primarily responsible for managing the financial risks of the corporation. This officer is also responsible for financial planning and record-keeping, as well as financial reporting to higher management. In some sectors, the CFO is also responsible for data analysis. The title is equivalent to finance director, a common title in the United Kingdom. The CFO typically reports to the CEO and to the board of directors, and may additionally sit on the board.

CIO Chief information officer, or IT director, is a job title commonly given to the most senior executive in an enterprise responsible for the IT and computer systems that support enterprise goals.

or

A chief innovation officer or CINO is a person in a company who "originates new ideas but also recognizes innovative ideas generated by other people." The term *chief innovation officer* was first coined and described in the 1998 book *Fourth Generation R&D*.

CMO A chief marketing officer (CMO) is a corporate executive responsible for marketing activities in an organization. Most often the CMO reports to the CEO.

cookie A cookie, also known as an HTTP cookie, Web cookie, or browser cookie, is usually a small piece of data sent from a website and stored in a user's Web browser while a user is browsing a website. When the user browses the same website in the future, the data stored in the cookie can be retrieved to notify the website administrator of the user's previous activity.

CPM Cost per impression, often abbreviated to CPI or CPM (cost per mille), is a term used in online advertising and marketing related to Web traffic. They refer to the cost of Internet marketing campaigns where advertisers pay for every time an ad is displayed, usually in the form of a banner ad on a website, but can also refer to advertisements in e-mail advertising.

CQ Adobe CQ Web Content Management (WCM) is a platform for delivering engaging, cross-channel customer experiences to drive online business success. Adobe CQ WCM provides a productive, easy-to-learn authoring environment with support for in-place editing; drag-and-drop page composition from a rich library of Web components; and intuitive controls for SEO, scheduled delivery, and landing page optimization including real-time A/B and multivariant tests.

CRM Customer relationship management (CRM) is a widely implemented model for managing a company's interactions with customers, clients, and sales prospects. It involves using technology to organize, automate, and synchronize business processes—principally sales activities, but also those for marketing, customer service, and technical support. The overall goals are to find, attract, and win new clients, service and retain those the company already has, entice former clients to return, and reduce the costs of marketing and client service.

crowdsourcing The concept of crowdsourcing has given way to the trend of user-generated advertisements. User-generated ads are created by consumers as opposed to an advertising agency or the company themselves; most often they are a result of brand-sponsored advertising competitions.

data/big data In IT, big data is a collection of data sets so large and complex that it becomes difficult to process using on-hand database management tools. The challenges include capture, curation, storage, search, sharing, analysis, and visualization.

digital out-of-home Digital out-of-home (DOOH) refers to dynamic media distributed across place-based networks in venues including, but not limited to cafes, bars, restaurants, health clubs, colleges, arenas, gas stations, and public spaces. DOOH networks typically feature independently addressable screens, kiosks, jukeboxes, and/or Jumbotrons. DOOH media benefits location owners and advertisers alike in being able to engage customers and/or audiences and extend the reach and effectiveness of marketing messages. It is also referred to as digital signage.

DSP (demand-side platform) A demand-side platform (DSP) is a system that allows digital advertisers to manage multiple ad exchange and data exchange accounts through one interface.

Real-time bidding for displaying online ads takes place within the ad exchanges; by utilizing a DSP, marketers can manage their bids for the banners and the pricing for the data that they are layering on to target their audiences. Much like paid search, using DSPs allows users to optimize based on set key performance indicators such as cost per click and cost per action.

DVR A digital video recorder (DVR), sometimes referred to by the merchandising term personal video recorder (PVR), is a consumer electronics device or application software that records video in a digital format to a disk drive, USB flash drive, SD memory card, or other local or networked mass storage device.

earned media Earned media (or free media) refers to favorable publicity gained through promotional efforts other than advertising, as opposed to paid media, which refers to publicity gained through advertising. Earned media often refers specifically to publicity gained through editorial influence, whereas social media refers to publicity gained through grassroots action, particularly on the Internet. The media may include any mass media outlets, such as newspaper, television, radio, and the Internet, and may include a variety of formats, such as news articles or shows, letters to the editor, editorials, and polls on television and the Internet.

EC2 Amazon Elastic Compute Cloud (EC2) is a central part of Amazon.com's cloud-computing platform, Amazon Web Services (AWS). EC2 allows users to rent virtual computers on which to run their own computer applications. EC2 allows scalable deployment of applications by providing a Web service through which a user can boot an Amazon Machine Image to create a virtual machine, which Amazon calls an instance, containing any software desired.

exabyte The exabyte (derived from the SI prefix *exa-*) is a unit of information or computer storage equal to 1 quintillion bytes (short scale). The unit symbol for the exabyte is EB. The unit prefix *exa-* indicates the sixth power of 1,000:

1EB = 1,000,000,000,000,000,000B = 10^{18} bytes = 1,000,000,000 gigabytes = 1,000,000 terabytes = 1,000 petabytes

experience design Experience design (XD) is the practice of designing products, processes, services, events, and environments with a focus placed on the quality of the user experience and culturally relevant solutions. An emerging discipline, experience design draws from many other disciplines including cognitive psychology and perceptual psychology, linguistics, cognitive science, architecture and environmental design, haptics, hazard analysis, product design, theatre, information design, information architecture, ethnography, brand strategy, interaction design, service design, storytelling, heuristics, technical communication, and design thinking.

Fluent A Razorfish-created digital marketing technology platform for marketers and agencies to target, distribute, and manage multichannel digital campaigns and experiences with a single, integrated software suite.

front-end Front-end and back-end, in addition to their obvious use in everyday English, are generalized terms that refer to the initial and the final stages of a process. The front-end is responsible for collecting input in various forms from the user and processing it to conform to a specification the back-end can use. The front-end is an interface between the user and the back-end.

Gen Y Generation Y, also known as the millennial generation, is the demographic cohort following Generation X. There are no precise dates for when Generation Y starts and ends. Commentators use beginning birth dates from the latter 1970s, or the early 1980s to the early 2000s (decade).

Google App Engine Google App Engine (often referred to as GAE or simply App Engine, and also used by the acronym GAE/J) is a platform as a service (PaaS) cloud-computing platform for developing and hosting Web applications in Google-managed data centers. Applications are sandboxed and run across multiple servers.

App Engine offers automatic scaling for Web applications; thus, as the number of requests increases for an application, App Engine automatically allocates more resources for the Web application to handle the additional demand.

Google Panda Google Panda is a change to Google's search results–ranking algorithm that was first released in February 2011. The change aimed at lowering the rank of "low-quality sites" or "thin sites," and returning higher-quality sites near the top of the search results. CNET reported a surge in the rankings of news websites and social networking sites and a drop in rankings for sites containing large amounts of advertising. This change reportedly affected the rankings of almost 12 percent of all search results.

GPS The global positioning system (GPS) is a space-based satellite navigation system that provides location and time information in all weather, anywhere on or near the Earth, where there is an unobstructed line of sight to four or more GPS satellites. It is maintained by the U.S. government and is freely accessible to anyone with a GPS receiver.

hackathon A hackathon (also known as a hack day, hackfest, or codefest) is an event in which computer programmers and others in the field of software development, such as graphic designers, interface designers, project managers, and computational philologists, collaborate intensively on software projects. Occasionally, there is a hardware component as well. Hackathons typically last between a day and a week.

Hadoop Apache Hadoop is an open-source software framework that supports data-intensive distributed applications, licensed under the Apache v2 license. It supports the running of applications on large clusters of commodity hardware. The Hadoop framework transparently provides both reliability and data motion for applications. Hadoop implements a computational paradigm named map/reduce, where the application is divided into many small fragments of work, each of which may be executed or reexecuted on any node in the cluster.

HTML HyperText Markup Language (HTML) is the main markup language for displaying Web pages and other information that can be displayed in a Web browser.

HTML5 HTML5 is a markup language for structuring and presenting content for the World Wide Web and a core technology of the Internet. It is the fifth revision of the HTML standard (created in 1990 and standardized as HTML4 as of 1997), and, as of December 2012, was still under development. Its core aims have been to improve the language with support for the latest multimedia while keeping it easily readable by humans and consistently understood by computers and devices (Web browsers, parsers, etc.). HTML5 is intended to subsume not only HTML 4 but XHTML 1 and DOM Level 2 HTML as well.

impressions An impression (in the context of online advertising) is a measure of the number of times an ad is displayed, whether it is clicked on or not. Each time an ad displays it is counted as one impression.

IDC International Data Corporation (IDC) is a market research, analysis, and advisory firm specializing in IT, telecommunications, and consumer technology. IDC is a wholly owned subsidiary of IDG. IDC is headquartered in Framingham, Massachusetts, and has more than 1,000 analysts worldwide covering technology and industry opportunities, trends, and forecasts in more than 110 countries. IDC's Insights line of businesses provide industry-focused advice for IT buyers in the financial, government, health, retail, manufacturing, and energy verticals.

iOS iOS (previously iPhone OS) is a mobile operating system developed and distributed by Apple Inc. Originally released in 2007 for the iPhone and iPod Touch, it has been extended to support other Apple devices such as the iPad and Apple TV. Unlike Microsoft's Windows Phone (Windows CE) and Google's Android, Apple does not license iOS for installation on non-Apple hardware.

IPO An initial public offering (IPO) or stock market launch is a type of public offering in which shares of stock in a company are sold to the general public on a securities exchange for the first time. Through this process, a private company transforms into a public company.

infrastructure as a service In this most basic cloud service model, infrastructure as a service (IaaS) providers offer computers as physical or more often as virtual machines, and other resources. The virtual machines are run as guests by a hypervisor, such as Xen or KVM. Pools of hypervisors within the cloud operational support system support large numbers of virtual machines and the ability to scale services up and down according to customers' varying requirements.

Kanban This is a method for developing software products and processes with an emphasis on just-in-time delivery while not overloading the software developers. In this approach, the process, from definition of a task to its delivery to the customer, is displayed for participants to see and developers pull work from a queue.

lean management Lean manufacturing, lean enterprise, or lean production, often simply lean, is a production practice that considers the expenditure of resources for any goal other than the creation of value for the end customer to be wasteful, and thus a target for elimination. Working from the perspective of the customer who consumes a product or service, *value* is defined as any action or process that a customer would be willing to pay for.

location-based services Location-based services (LBS) are a general class of computer program-level services used to include specific controls for location and time data as control features in computer programs. As such, LBS is information and has a number of uses in social networking today as an entertainment service, which is accessible with mobile devices through the mobile network and which uses information on the geographical position of the mobile device. This has become more and more important with the expansion of the smartphone and tablet markets as well.

lovemarks Lovemarks are a marketing concept that is intended to replace the idea of brands. The idea was first widely publicized in a book of the same name written by Kevin Roberts, CEO of the advertising agency Saatchi & Saatchi. In the book Roberts claims, "Brands are running out of juice." He considers that love is what is needed to rescue brands.

media fragmentation Media fragmentation refers to the increasing availability and consumption of different types of media across channels.

MLB Major League Baseball (MLB) is a professional baseball league, consisting of teams that play in the American League and the National League. After 100 years as separate legal entities, the two leagues merged in 2000 into a single organization led by the Commissioner of Baseball.

Möbius strip The Möbius strip or Möbius band (UK/'mɜrbiəs/ or US/'moʊbiəs/; from German 'mø:bi̯ʊs), also Mobius or Moebius, is a surface with only one side and only one boundary component. The Möbius strip has the mathematical property of being nonorientable. It can be realized as a ruled surface. It was discovered independently by the German mathematicians August Ferdinand Möbius and Johann Benedict Listing in 1858.

Moore's law Moore's law is the observation that over the history of computing hardware, the number of transistors on integrated circuits doubles approximately every two years. The period often quoted as "18 months" is due to Intel executive David House, who predicted that period for a doubling in chip performance (being a combination of the effect of more transistors and their being faster).

native advertising Native advertising is defined as ad strategies that allow brands to promote their content into the endemic experience of a website or app. Native ad experiences differ from traditional digital ad formats such as display and preroll because they are well integrated to the visual design of a publisher's site and are choice based, meaning that they do not rely on interruptive or distracting mechanisms to force a user's attention.

Native advertising exists in many different formats, including promoted videos, images, articles, music, and other media types. The consistent attributes of native ads across all of these types of media follow: strong visual integration with the publisher's look and feel; choice-based interaction; and content-based experiences. That is, ads are experienced as stand-alone content, not attached to unrelated media on the site.

omnichannel Omnichannel retailing is very similar to, and an evolution of, multichannel retailing, but is concentrated more on a seamless approach to the consumer experience through all available shopping channels, that is, mobile Internet devices, computers, brick-and-mortar, television, catalog, and so on. The omnichannel consumer wants to use all channels simultaneously, and retailers using an omnichannel approach will track customers across all channels, not just one or two. Using omnichannel retailing while working with the "connected consumer," all shopping channels work from the same database of products, prices, promotions, and so on. Instead of perceiving a variety of touchpoints as part of the same brand, omnichannel retailers let consumers experience the brand, not a channel within a brand.

Open API Open API (often referred to as OpenAPI new technology) is a word used to describe sets of technologies that enable websites to interact with each other by using REST, SOAP, JavaScript and other Web technologies. Although its possibilities aren't limited to Web-based applications, it's becoming an increasing trend in so-called Web 2.0 applications.

open hardware platform Open architecture is a type of computer architecture or software architecture that is designed to make adding, upgrading, and swapping components easy. For example, the IBM PC and Apple IIe have an open architecture supporting plug-in cards, whereas the Apple IIc and Amiga 500 computers have a closed architecture. In a closed architecture, the hardware manufacturer chooses the components, and they are not generally intended to be upgraded by the end user.

open-source software Open-source software (OSS) is computer software available with source code. The source code and certain other rights normally reserved for copyright holders are provided under an open-source license that permits users to study, change, improve, and also at times to distribute the software.

OS An operating system (OS) is a collection of software that manages computer hardware resources and provides common services for computer programs. The OS is a vital component of the system software in a computer system. Application programs usually require an OS to function.

owned media Owned media is a media channel that the publisher owns, such as a business website, social media account, or YouTube channel. Typically, owned media means that the owner can publish virtually whatever type of content on the channel he or she chooses. The term is usually used in connection with paid media and earned media.

paid media Promotional efforts gained publicly by spending money to leverage a channel.

PDF Portable document format (PDF) is a file format used to represent documents in a manner independent of application software, hardware, and operating systems. Each PDF file encapsulates a complete description of a fixed-layout flat document, including the text, fonts, graphics, and other information needed to display it.

petabyte A petabyte (derived from the SI prefix *peta-*) is a unit of information equal to 1 quadrillion (short scale) bytes, or 1 billiard (long-scale) bytes. The unit symbol for the petabyte is PB. The prefix *peta-* (P) indicates the fifth power to 1,000:

$1\text{PB} = 1{,}000{,}000{,}000{,}000{,}000\text{B} = 1{,}000^5\text{B} = 10^5\text{B} =$ 1million gigabytes = 1,000,000 terabytes = 1,000 terabytes

platform as a service Platform as a service (PaaS) is a category of cloud computing services that provides a computing platform and a solution stack as a service. Along with software as a service (SaaS) and infrastructure as a service (IaaS), it is a service model of cloud computing. In this model, the consumer creates the software using tools and/or libraries from the provider. The consumer also controls software deployment and configuration settings. The provider provides the networks, servers, storage, and other services.

platform technology Platform technology is a term for technology that enables the creation of products and processes that support present or future development. It establishes the long-term capabilities of research and development institutes. It can be defined as a structural or technological form from which various products can emerge without the expense of a new process/technology introduction.

POS system Point of sale (POS) or checkout is the place where a transaction occurs in exchange for goods or services. The POS often refers to the physical electronic cash register or dedicated POS hardware used for checkout, but the POS is simply the location where the sale is conducted, money changes hands, and a receipt is given, which can also occur on a smartphone, tablet, laptop, or mobile POS device when the right hardware and POS software is combined with the mobile device.

procurement Procurement is the acquisition of goods or services. It is favorable that the goods/services are appropriate and that they are procured at the best possible cost to meet the needs of the purchaser in terms of quality and quantity, time, and location. Corporations and public bodies often define processes intended to promote fair and open competition for their business while minimizing exposure to fraud and collusion.

QR code QR code (abbreviated from quick response code) is the trademark for a type of matrix barcode (or two-dimensional code) first designed for the automotive industry. More recently, the system has become popular outside the industry due to its fast readability and large storage capacity compared to standard UPC barcodes.

RFID Radio-frequency identification (RFID) is the use of a wireless noncontact system that uses radio-frequency electromagnetic fields to transfer data from a tag attached to an object for the purposes of automatic identification and tracking. Some tags require no battery and are powered and read at short ranges via magnetic fields (electromagnetic induction).

ROI Return on investment (ROI), or rate of return (ROR), also known as rate of profit or sometimes just return, is the ratio of money gained or lost (whether realized or unrealized) on an investment relative to the amount of money invested.

RSS Rich Site Summary (RSS, originally RDF Site Summary, often dubbed Really Simple Syndication) is a family of Web feed formats used to publish frequently updated works—such as blog entries, news headlines, audio, and video—in a standardized format. An RSS document (which is called a feed, Web feed, or channel) includes full or summarized text, plus metadata such as publishing dates and authorship.

RTB Real-time bidding (RTB) is a relatively new method of selling and buying online display advertising in real time, one ad impression at a time.

S3 Amazon S3 (Simple Storage Service) is an online storage Web service offered by Amazon Web Services. Amazon S3 provides storage through Web services interfaces (REST, SOAP, and BitTorrent). Amazon launched S3—its first publicly available Web service—in the United States in March 2006 and in Europe in November 2007.

Salesforce Salesforce.com Inc., is a global enterprise software company headquartered in San Francisco, California. Although best known for its customer relationship management (CRM) product, Salesforce has also expanded into the social enterprise arena through acquisitions. It was ranked number 27 in *Fortune*'s 100 Best Companies to Work for in 2012.

scrum Scrum is an iterative and incremental Agile software development framework for managing software projects and product or application development. Scrum has not only reinforced interest in project management but also challenged conventional ideas about such management. Scrum focuses on project management institutions where it is difficult to plan ahead. Mechanisms of empirical process control, where feedback loops that constitute the core management technique are used as opposed to traditional command-and-control-oriented management.

scrum master Scrum is facilitated by a scrum master, who is accountable for removing impediments to the ability of the team to deliver the sprint goal/deliverables. The scrum master is not the team leader, but acts as a buffer between the team and any distracting influences. The scrum master ensures that the scrum process is used as intended. The scrum master is the enforcer of rules. A key part of the scrum master's role is to protect the development team and keep it focused on the tasks at hand. The role has also been referred to as a servant-leader to reinforce these dual perspectives.

search engine A Web search engine is designed to search for information on the World Wide Web. The search results are generally presented in a line of results often referred to as search engine results pages (SERPs). The information may be specialized in Web pages, images, information, and other types of files. Some search engines also mine data available in databases or open directories.

SKU A stock-keeping unit or SKU (/'skju:/ or /.ɛs.keI'ju:/) is a number or code used to identify each unique product or item for sale in a store or other business.

It is a unique identifier for each distinct product and service that can be purchased.

software as a service Software as a service (SaaS, pronounced sæs or sas), sometimes referred to as on-demand software, is a software delivery model in which software and associated data are centrally hosted on the cloud. SaaS is typically accessed by users using a thin client via a Web browser.

Sprint A sprint is the basic unit of development in scrum. Sprints last between one week and one month, and they are a "timeboxed" (i.e., restricted to a specific duration) effort of a constant length.

Each sprint is preceded by a planning meeting, where the tasks for the sprint are identified and an estimated commitment for the sprint goal is made, and followed by a review or retrospective meeting at which the progress is reviewed and lessons for the next sprint are identified.

Square Square is an electronic payment service, provided by Square Inc. Square allows users in the United States and Canada to accept credit cards through their mobile phones, either by swiping the card on the Square device or by manually entering the details on the phone. In August 2012, Starbucks announced it would start using Square to process transactions with customers who pay via debit or credit card. The corporation will also reportedly invest $25 million in Square Inc., with Starbucks CEO Howard Schultz becoming a board member of the company.

streaming media Streaming media is multimedia that is constantly received by and presented to an end user while being delivered by a provider. Its verb form, "to stream," refers to the process of delivering media in this manner; the term refers to the delivery method of the medium rather than the medium itself.

system integrators A systems integrator is a person or company that specializes in bringing together component subsystems into a whole and ensuring that those subsystems function together, a practice known as system integration. Systems integrators may work in many fields but the term is generally used in the IT field, the defense industry, or in media.

terabyte The terabyte is a multiple of the unit byte digital information. The prefix *tera-* means 10^{12} in the International System of Units (SI), and therefore 1 terabyte is 1,000,000,000,000 bytes, or 1 trillion (short-scale) bytes, or 1,000 gigabytes. One terabyte in binary prefixes is 0.9095 tebibytes, or 931.32 gibibytes. The unit symbol for the terabyte is TB or TByte, but not Tb (lowercase b), which refers to terabit.

TVB Founded in 1953, the Television Bureau of Advertising (TVB) is a private nonprofit association for the commercial television industry in the United States.

ubicomp Ubiquitous computing (ubicomp) is a post-desktop model of human-computer interaction in which information processing has been thoroughly integrated into everyday objects and activities. In the course of ordinary activities, individuals "using" ubicomp engages many computational devices and systems simultaneously, and may not necessarily even be aware that they are doing so. This model is considered an advancement from the older desktop paradigm. More formally, *ubicomp* is defined as "machines that fit the human environment instead of forcing humans to enter theirs."

upfronts In the North American television industry, an upfront is a meeting hosted at the start of important advertising sales periods by television network executives, and attended by the press and major advertisers. It is so named because of its main purpose, which is to allow marketers to buy television commercial airtime "up front," or several months before the television season begins.

USB Universal serial bus (USB) is an industry standard developed in the mid-1990s that defines the cables, connectors, and communications protocols used in a bus for connection, communication, and power supply between computers and electronic devices.

VC Venture capital (VC) is financial capital provided to early-stage, high-potential, high-risk growth startup companies. The VC fund makes money by owning equity in the companies it invests in, which usually have a novel technology or business model in high-technology industries, such as biotechnology, IT, software, and so on. The typical VC investment occurs after the seed funding round as a growth funding round (also referred to as series A round) in the interest of generating a return through an eventual realization event, such as an IPO or trade sale of the company. Venture capital is a subset of private equity. Therefore, all VC is private equity, but not all private equity is VC.

Waterfall process The waterfall model is a sequential design process, often used in software development processes, in which progress is seen as flowing steadily downward (like a waterfall) through the phases of conception, initiation, analysis, design, construction, testing, production/implementation, and maintenance.

zettabyte A zettabyte (symbol ZB, derived from the SI prefix *zetta-*) is a quantity of information or information storage capacity equal to 10^{21} bytes or 1,000 exabytes (or 1 sextillion [one long-scale trilliard] bytes).

Acknowledgments

We've worked together for more than a decade, which is several lifetimes in technology years. Now, as CEO and CTO of Razorfish, we want to share what we have learned about the present and future of technology, creativity, and marketing.

It's fitting that a book about convergence has many authors. Although our names are on the cover, the content has been shaped by countless clients, colleagues, and competitors.

We thank all Fish, past and present. As with much of creation, this work is in part a synthesis that comes from a lot of great thinking and collaboration across Razorfish and with our partner network.

We thank all clients, past and present. We, of course, wouldn't be writing this book without those clients, who on a daily basis impress us with their boldness and their courage. Being a marketing executive in this day and age isn't an easy job, and we're lucky to call some of the best in the business partners, clients, and even friends. (We extend extra appreciation to the clients who allowed us to interview them for this manuscript.)

Outside the marketing and technology worlds, there are many people we wish to thank. From a very young age, Bob was taught that life has many lessons that come through only when you live it to its fullest and when you are open to learning continuously. Bob's family has given him the courage to learn, push the boundaries of what is possible, and then learn some more. Ray's parents were instrumental in the development of a burgeoning CTO when they encouraged and supported a nerdy 10-year-old's fascination with computers—way before it was deemed wise to do so.

To our children, Emily, Drew, and Paige Lord and Ramon and Veronica Velez, for teaching us about the freshness of the digital world. Drew's exclusive use of Google Docs, Emily's rejection of e-mail at age 15, Paige's early identification of Instagram (before Facebook knew of its existence), Ramon's maker ornament that got us soldering a microcontroller, and watching Veronica dance with her Robosapien. In their own way, they have helped us understand the consumer of the future. Just like a technology petri dish within our own homes.

Last but certainly not least, we'd like to thank our wives, Robin and Cherith, who have indulged us during countless hours staring at laptops and on countless nights away on business. Without their support, our success would have been impossible, impractical, and empty.

Index